DUNIA

A GARDEN IN THE GULAG

GILLIAN CALDWELL

For my mother, who has always been there for me.

&

For the healing of my ancestral line, in all directions.

"Give me your blessing, mother, I seek a root, an herb to cure the insanity of men."

— *PAVLO TYCHYNA, 1918*

CONTENTS

Preface 9

1. 1904: Childhood 11
2. 1908: The Family Trade 19
3. 1909: Music 25
4. 1913: Love 34
5. 1914: A Wedding 42
6. 1918: Family 47
7. 1918: Political Unrest 52
8. 1918: Harvest 57
9. 1918: Winter 65
10. 1925: Ivan 72
11. 1928: Political Shift 76
12. 1930: Maroushka 83
13. 1931: September 88
14. 1932: November 96
15. 1932: December 105
16. 1932: The Journey North 115
17. 1933: Kobeliaky 122
18. 1933: The Gulag 128
19. 1933: Dunia's 22nd day in the Gulag 133
20. 1933: Holodomor 138
21. 1933: Holodomor; Ivan (14) 142
22. 1933: Dunia 149
23. 1933: Garden in Siberia 154
24. 1933: The Dream 159
25. 1934: Planting Seeds 161
26. 1934: The Experimental Farm 165
27. 1935: October 171
28. 1935: Christmas 177
29. The Wind Shifts 183
30. 1936: The Island of Prorva 189
31. Water 194

32. The Natives 199
33. Death 204
34. Khazars 208
35. God 211
36. Allah 216
37. Goodbye 221
38. The Ship 227
39. 1938: The Great Purge 233
40. 1939: The Professor 238
41. The River 245
42. Another Place 250
43. Burying the past 256
44. The Truck 262
45. The Authorities, 1939 268
46. The Search 275
Epilogue 281

Words of Gratitude 284
Author Bio 285

PREFACE

This is the story of my great-grandmother, Dunia. It was handed down to me through my grandfather, Ivan, whose voice my mother recorded and later transcribed. She also helped me piece together the timeline and construct the family tree. Throughout this journey, I consulted her often, striving to remain as faithful as possible to Dunia's story.

I call this a work of fiction because I've painted the landscapes, filled in the gaps, and imagined characters to bring the story to life as I envision it might have been. Along the way, I felt the presence of my ancestors, guiding and sharing their wisdom with me.

This book is my way of honoring them and their legacy.

FAMILY TREE

- **Maroushka**
  - **Nepephan** married **Katya**
    - Their children (oldest to youngest):
      - **Anichka**
      - **Nickolai**
      - **Krystyan**
      - **Sveta**
      - **Mykhailo**
      - **Lyaksandro**
      - **Dunia**
        - Dunia married **Jacob**
          - Their children (oldest to youngest):
          - **Marta**
          - **Katerina**
          - **Ivan**
          - **Andrei**
          - **Alex**
          - **The twins** (never named)
          - **Mary**

1

1904: CHILDHOOD

9 YEARS OLD

Dunia sings to the sheep, the sheep bleat back. They know her voice, they know her scent and they trust her. The flock wanders up the hillside, decorated with corn-flower and mallow and nibbles its way through grass and weeds to the edge of the woods. Oak, Ash, Hornbeam and a variety of shrubs make up the place the children refer to as Zelenyy Lis[1]. The sheep stop and drink from a lively brook that bubbles and chatters past. From her shady spot under an Ash tree, Dunia chews on a blade of grass and looks down and across the field at the village of Kobelyiaky.

The village is a collection of white-washed huts and gardens bursting with late summer produce – green beans, cabbage, potatoes and beets. Horses, pigs and sheep laze and graze in paddocks and pens while chickens roam freely, pecking at this and that, making a meal out of grain and grub. Larger homesteads pepper the country-side surrounding the village.

1. The Green Forest

Wheat, barley and millet grow here in the rich black soil, weaving the scene into a golden-green patch-work quilt.

The villagers make their living from earth and beast. They feed themselves and their neighbors, trading harvest and tools among themselves. One family's life blends and extends to the next, with parents looking out for their neighbor's children and the children calling any number of the village grandmothers "Baba[2]."

Dunia continues to sing. The tune is filled in and rounded out with bird-song, sheep-song and the sound of the breeze blowing through Zelenyy Lis.

Dunia is the youngest of seven children to her father, Nepefan and her mother, Katya. Nepefan's mother lives with them too. Her name is Maroushka but the children call her Baba. From oldest to youngest, the children are Anichka, Nickolai, Krystyan, Sveta, Mykhailo, Lyaksandro and Dunia. They live in a cozy hut with dirt floors. There's a sheep pen in the front surrounded by a wooden fence and a vegetable garden in the back. The family makes a living off the land and their sheep, using wool to create beautiful woven carpets. Family-life is busy and no one is too old or too young to contribute to planting and harvesting the garden, feeding the chickens, tending and shearing the sheep or spinning yarn and weaving carpets that are later sold to the villagers or at market.

Most of these jobs have a season and are assigned by the natural order. It's based on each family member's strength, natural ability and desire. Of course there are the jobs that

2. Grandmother

no one wants to do and those are usually delegated by Nepefan.

As the youngest child, Dunia takes care of the sheep. This job calls for patience and a soft touch but doesn't require a lot of strength, so it's best carried out by a child or a grandparent. Maroushka shares the task with Dunia when she isn't busy at her regular post, preparing meals and puttering around the kitchen and the garden with Katya.

During the summer, most of the cooking is done outside in the yard. Dunia often sees Maroushka sitting on a stump near the garden, paring vegetables, a pile of peelings gathered around her feet. Nepefan, Krystian and Mykhailo had built a Piche[3] two summers ago, following the techniques Nepefan had learned from his Father.

There is a second Piche inside the hut that Nepefan built himself. It doubles as a fire-place and a heater. He built a sturdy shelf above it that could be slept on. It's a good use of space and it makes for a cozy and coveted spot during the winter months. Cooking is indoors or outdoors in harmony with the season. And for the most part, the indoor piche remains fallow during the summer.

For sixteen years Maroushka and Katya have shared the kitchen and this time together has smoothed out some of their rougher edges. They've learned each other's ways and weaknesses and, for the most part, come to an understanding. Maroushka takes a deep breath and swallows her pride

3. Clay oven – (pronounced peech) a traditional masonry oven dating back to the 15th century used for cooking, baking and when built indoors, as a fireplace for heating.

when Katya lets out an exasperated puff of air and says, "I think it's time for you to go take care of the sheep for a while now."

Maroushka wipes her hands on her apron, puts on her boots and heads out to the field in search of Dunia. Maroushka can hear Dunia's song blowing in on the wind. She heads up toward the brook. Dunia is always singing. She makes up tunes and verses; they consume her. She sings in the garden and out in the field. She sings to the sheep and to the other children. One day Nikolai, Dunia's older brother, complained during supper because the neighbor's daughter had overheard *him* singing Dunia's song while he was shearing the sheep.

Maroushka finds Dunia chewing on a blade of cat grass and watering the sheep near the brook. She sits down to catch her breath. "Did Mamo send you out?" Dunia asks.

"Tak[4], she had enough of Baba."

They sit together for a moment taking in the sweet air. Dunia cuddles up to Maroushka. Baba has a distinct smell. She smells like the kitchen- potatoes, beets and smoke, and the earth and a touch of cedar and a hint of sweat. Dunia hums her song and Maroushka hums along. They sit side by side for a long time. The afternoon is warming up and Maroushka can smell wild strawberries on the breeze. "Let's pick some berries, I'll show you a good patch," she says.

They get up, brush the grass from their dresses and herd the sheep toward Zelenyy Lis to nibble on the greens and

---

4. Yes

flowers that grow there. Maroushka leads the way to an abundant patch of strawberries. The sweet fragrance makes Dunia's mouth water. Together, they bend down and begin to fill their apron pockets. Dunia pops a small handful of the berries into her mouth. This is her berry picking policy, 'I eat as I go,' she thinks. The berries are warm from the sun and bursting with sweetness. She stands up for a moment and closes her eyes, lost in a symphony of flavor. When she opens her eyes again, she sees Baba looking up at her.

Dunia smiles, her cheeks bloom and the shade of her lips give her away. Baba smiles, her lips are a brighter shade of pink too.

Baba gathers all of the berries from Dunia's apron into her own apron pocket and releases Dunia from her task for the afternoon; she is free to play with her friends. Dunia kisses Baba goodbye and runs off through the field, past a grove of trees toward the river.

The Voorskla River flows beside the village. It is gentle and meandering this time of year and plants and minerals give it a copper color. The children gather and splash at the water's edge. One of the village boys, Peder, who is five years old, is already knee deep and elbow deep in the mud. He's bent at the waist, arms submerged, stirring and kneading the muck. He stands up and yells, "I am the mud man!" throwing his muddy arms in the air and flinging mud all around him. This sends the other children scampering off in all directions. The throng of children, about twelve of them, spend the day exploring inlets and swimming holes, catching fish and other creatures, climbing the banks, digging holes, hiding, seeking and eventually full submersion, floating on their backs down-stream, staring upwards at the clouds. The river is a natural playground and no one is clean or dry as they head back through the fields and toward the village that evening.

Dunia goes to the back of the hut and finds Maroushka setting the table for supper. "Can you bring me my other dress?" she asks. The old woman nods and disappears into the house for a minute. Dunia sits on the stump next to the garden and examines her grubby feet. Maroushka returns carrying a plate of Kartoplianyky[5] in her hand and the dress tucked under her arm. She hands the dress to Dunia and makes her way to the big wooden table in the yard. This is where the family eats their meals when the weather is warm. Dunia hangs her wet clothes on the line. She washes her hands and feet in a bucket of water. Then she scurries over to the table to see what's for supper.

The family gathers together and Katya serves up steaming bowls of green Borscht[6] made from duck stock, beetroot, potatoes, hard boiled eggs chopped into pieces and sorrel that grows wild in the fields. The table is arranged with sour cream, pickled vegetables and Kartoplianyky. A small bowl covered by a cloth contains the wild strawberries she and Maroushka had collected earlier. They'll be served for dessert with fresh cream from the neighbor's cow.

Dunia loves to eat.

"It's the only time she stops singing," her brother Nikolai often says, with a display of exaggerated relief.

---

5. fried potato cakes
6. a sour soup made with beets, carrots, potatoes and cabbage

When Dunia sits down to eat, she gets a serious look on her face as she explores the flavors and textures of her meal. She becomes focused on the bite at hand and often misses the first half of dinner conversation, lost in the enchantment of her meal.

Afterward, her belly warm and her hunger sated, she sits back with a look of contentment. Dunia listens now as her father shares about his day.

Nepefan is an educated man and he spends some of his time teaching the village children their numbers and letters. Groups of ten or twelve children gather on the living-room carpet, faces turned upwards to Nepefan as he shares the day's lesson. Sometimes their studies take them outside into the garden - with the little ones counting cabbages or bugs and the older children reading passages from literature and poetry trying to decipher their meaning. He generously passes his knowledge on to his children saying "They're never too young to learn." Dunia has known how to read and write from the age of six.

That night, before bed, Dunia reads out loud from a small, leather-bound bible with gold rimmed pages. It belonged to her grandfather, who died when she was little. She doesn't remember him but feels like she knows him after hours and hours spent listening to Maroushka's stories about the man. Maroushka says that when they were young, and before the war, he used to make her laugh until she cried. Dunia treasures the little book and loves to flip slowly through its soft pages, admiring their golden edges. She keeps it tucked away in the wall side corner of her mattress. Dunia reads out loud,

"Let the little children come to me, and do not hinder them, for the kingdom of heaven belongs to such as these."

2

1908: THE FAMILY TRADE

12 YEARS OLD

It's spring in Kobelyiaky and the land is bursting with new life. Bright green grass shoots up from the earth. This is the first, hope-filled sign of a welcome new season. Before the last of the snow melted, a few brave crocuses poked their fuzzy little heads tentatively out from the ground like a question, 'Is the worst over now?'

Siberian squill and snowdrops were the next to make their debut. After this, the flood gates open and the flowers and herbs come up in patches. They decorate the landscape with colors that shift daily, like living art. One variety of flower fades out, giving way to the glory of the next. Maroushka, spends her afternoons walking the fields. She is looking for something.

One evening, she bustles into the hut before supper. Katya is topping and tailing some wrinkled spring greens into a bowl. Maroushka hangs her scarf on a hook near the door and turns with excitement. "They're ready," she says, raising her hands in the air and doing a little dance with her feet, "We start tomorrow."

The next day, Maroushka, Dunia and her two older sisters, Anichka and Sveta, set out early. They spend the morning gathering plants, petals, herbs, roots and bark. These are the raw ingredients needed to create vegetable dyes. The family will use these to bring color to their woven carpets. The secrets of this art form have been passed down from generation to generation through Maroushka's line. Maroushka knows the land surrounding Kobelyiaky more intimately than anyone.

She takes the girls out on an adventure, beyond the vegetable garden and south through the fields. Here they collect wild chamomile, used to make yellow dye. "Let's fill the basket," Maroushka says. She is down on her knees picking the flower heads, "Katya wants extra for tea."

They take a long circuitous route, heading east around the village and through the quiet woods where they find madder root for red dye and woad flowers for blue. Maroushka shows them how to identify the plants and herbs by their leaves and points out the various landmarks that help her to navigate the land; an ancient oak that has been struck by lightning, a dry creek-bed, the remnants of an old shack and a massive white stone posing in the middle of a grassy field. They come to the Voorskla River where the knotweed abounds. The roots run deep, taking over the banks from here and north along the shore towards the next village. These leaves will be boiled gently to create a fresh green dye.

The clouds have been gathering all morning. "It's going to rain," Dunia says as she follows Maroushka through the front fields to Zelenyy Lis. Here, in the dim forest, they harvest oak bark for an earthy brown dye and wild carnations for a softer shade of yellow. Elderberries grow here too and they make a glorious purple dye but the fruit isn't ready until late July or early August. The berries make a delicious dessert and can also be preserved in their own juices and enjoyed into the winter.

"We need to go back now," Maroushka says, scanning the dark clouds. As they scurry back across the field, the sky opens up and big fat raindrops splash down on them. Dunia screams and a perfectly timed roll of thunder grumbles in response. Sveta pulls her shawl up over her head, balancing her baskets precariously on her arms. They hurry past the sheep pen where the sheep huddle together. The animals sway with the weight of their winter coats as the raindrops roll off of them and gather into a puddle at their feet. Dunia imagines the sheep are happy that Nickolai and Kristiyan put off shearing for another week. The girls pour into the hut, followed by Maroushka. They bring a cloud of fresh air with them. They smell like flowers and greens and earth and rain. Dunia's cheeks are like apples. The hut is warm and Katya stokes the fire in the oven. They put the baskets off to one side and lay their wet clothing out to dry. The afternoon will be spent refining raw ingredients into a rainbow.

The rain falls steadily and the hut is warm and steamy. Last year's wool hangs from the ceiling in tightly wound bundles. It is a natural white, ready to be dyed. The spinning and weaving is mostly completed in the winter months when the days are short and bitterly cold.

Maroushka stirs knotweed leaves into a big pot on the fire and gently brings them to a boil. Anichka stands at her side and assists. She leans in and listens as Maroushka speaks softly, almost as if she is speaking to the dye itself. Maroushka shares what she learned from her mother - the secrets to creating bright, rich color from these earthly ingredients. Nothing Maroushka says is new to Anichka. She's eighteen now and she's been a part of the process since she was a little girl but everything is about to change. Anichka is getting married in the fall and will move south to be with her husband's family. This will be her last time dyeing wool as a child and she feels it as an ache wrapped around her heart. "Shhhh," she hisses at Dunia, who has begun to sing loudly, "I need to hear this."

Katya and Sveta prepare the spun wool in a solution that will fix the color, while Nepefan sits in the corner, quietly working the loom. He's using up the end of last year's wool, including the purple elderberry wool, which is Dunia's favorite. Dunia stands behind Nepefan resting her hand on his shoulder and watching the geometric pattern take shape. It's a horizontal loom and he works it with speed and accuracy defined by years of practice. It's hypnotizing to watch. As Dunia watches, she sings. It's a new song and Dunia works it this way and that way, putting lyrics to melody. The rain has slowed to a trickle and Katya opens the door to let the fresh air in. The clouds are clearing up and the earth is drinking up the moisture. They lay the first batch of wool outside on the line, to dry. They get into a rhythm and the hut hums with the flow of their labor and the murmur of their voices.

The house is quieter than usual with the boys away at market. Lyaksandro is still a year younger than his brothers had been their first year at the spring market but he had begged to go with them and Nepefan had agreed, telling Nikolai, "you look out for him." They borrowed the neighbor's wagon, packed it with the remaining carpets from last season and left before the sun was up that morning. This was the first year they had gone without Nepefan, and Katya worried that they were cold and wet, or worse. As day eases into evening, their work tapers off - Katya and Maroushka begin to prepare supper while Anichka and Sveta wrap up the loose ends of the dyeing process. There is plenty more to do but it will have to wait for tomorrow. Dunia is working the loom now, fingers moving in and out completing her father's pattern. Nepefan heads out to chop wood and when he opens the door, he can hear talking and yelling in the distance.

"The boys are home!" he bellows as he goes out to meet them. Katya sighs deeply, dries her hands and goes outside to greet her sons on the path. The noise grows louder as they approach, shouting their victory.

"We sold all of it," Nikolai shouts as he approaches. He scans Nepefan's face. Katya and Nepefan approach the wagon to get a closer look. There are several new items that have been accepted in trade, including a bottle of Horilka[1] and fabric for ne[illegible] dresses. Dunia squeals when she sees the fabric. The [illegible] untered a bouquet of pheasant on the journey [illegible] Krystiyan, who is a natural hunter, showed [illegible] Lyaksandro how to capture them alive.

[illegible] ge, strong spirits, like Vodka.

Lyaksandro is out in front, proudly holding a wooden cage. He lifts it in the air like a trophy and brandishes the plump birds with a cocky smile.

Later that evening, as day fades into night, the family sits together in the hut. The conversation has softened to a murmur and Maroushka is falling asleep in her chair. Lyaksandro is fighting sleep too as he stares into the flames dancing in the hearth. Nepefan takes his Balalaika[2] from its place on the wall and plays it by fire-light. Dunia sits on the carpet by his feet and watches his fingers move along the strings. He strums a song and Katya sings along. The song is about a child that stays out past dark, gets lost in the woods and makes a bed in a hollowed out tree. Dunia can see the story playing out in her imagination. Next, Anichka requests her favorite, the one about the little bunny boy. It sounds like it should be a happy tune but the melody is sad and filled with longing. Sveta has a beautiful wooden whistle that Nepefan carved for her, called a *Sopilka.* She plays a wedding song and Dunia puts a scarf over her head and flutters her eyelashes, pretending to be a bride. Next, Dunia shares her new song with the family. Even Nikolai seems to enjoy it. Afterwards, Dunia sits mesmerized by the fire. Nepefan looks at her glowing face for a long time before he says, "Let's take a walk to St Vladimir's tomorrow, I think you should join the church choir."

---

2. a stringed instrument with a hollow triangular wooden body.

3

1909: MUSIC

13 YEARS OLD

"Olena is waiting by the gate!" Katya shouts toward the back field. Dunia is invisible to her mother from where she is, bent at the waist picking herbs and flowers. She stands up at the sound of her mother's voice, her head poking up suddenly out of the low shrubs and high grasses.

"Coming!" she shouts, skipping homeward.

Before she rounds the hut, she organizes what she's carrying and hides her hands behind her back.

"Pick one," she says, walking up to her friend, who is leaning against the fence and looking at the sheep.

Olena is used to this game. She points to Dunia's right hand. Dunia produces a purple flower and holds it out for her friend. Olena receives it with a smile.

"And," Dunia says playfully, showing her other hand. She is clutching a fragrant bouquet of herbs.

Olena looks at her questioningly.

"It's for your throat," Dunia says. "Maroushka told me peppermint tea is very soothing for a sore throat."

"Thank you!" Olena says, putting her hand to her throat and remembering their last conversation.

"If we're going to be singers, we have to take impeccable care of our instruments," Dunia says formally, imitating Zhanna Belovol, the choir director at St. Vladimir's Church.

The girls look at each other for a moment and break into laughter.

"Bye Mom!" Dunia shouts toward the hut. The girls turn and walk up the lane, in the direction of the church.

The church choir meets Tuesday evenings to practice. The girls walk there together. They are the same age and their voices blend well together. Dunia's voice is bright, like the sun, a warm yellow, orange sound, whereas Olena's voice has a deep, rich tone – dark purple, like elderberries. The two girls have known each other for years but sharing a relish for music has fastened their friendship.

"Let's sing the one about the sheep," Dunia says, admiring the red and orange poppies that have sprung up along the side of the road. Olena nods and Dunia hums the starting note. The girls link arms and sing as they walk.

"If today you hear God's voice,
harden not your hearts.
He is our God, and we are the people of His
pasture,
the sheep under His care."

Mr. Slenko, the neighbor down the lane, hears the girls singing in harmony. He stops his work in the field and leans against his shovel to listen. His wife is listening too, framed by the doorway of their hut. The Slenkos are used to hearing the girls pass by on Tuesday evenings and husband and wife share a smile before returning to their tasks.

The girls continue down the road, unaware that they've been heard. Their voices rise and fall. When they sing the chorus for the last time, they come to a stop. Dunia and Olena face each other. They slow the song down and look each other in the face. This is something Ms. Belovol has taught them to do, to perfect their harmonies. When the song is complete, the girls smile at one another.

"We sound good!" Olena says.

"Like angels," Dunia adds, clasping her hands together and looking up to the heavens.

They continue their walk in silence. An army of frogs croak a calm and steady chorus from Galena's pond. The sun is low in the sky, stretching the girls' shadows out long behind them. Dunia squints in the direction of the church.

She remembers being very small, maybe four years old, sitting at her father's feet in the garden, listening to Bible passages. She would scoop up the soil and let it run through her fingers as her father read. She remembers the images she had in her mind of the places in those stories and the people living out their lives in holy and unholy ways. Dunia swore she would be one of the good people, living her life out in the right way. She felt her first connection to God around this time – four years old. She felt it through her dad, through his words and the low rumble of his voice. She felt it through those stories and passages, through the soil and the plants in the garden and then later, through church. She has attended church all of her life, but the sight of St. Vladimir's means more to her now than it did before. It's because of music. This is where she gets to sing and create harmonies and learn how to read music. It's her favorite place to be, besides home or Zelenyy Lis or the river. She admires the building as she approaches. It's made up of sandstone and red brick, with a lofty spire and a stone stairway leading up to its double doors. There is a massive oak tree out front and fragrant lilac bushes along the side and a cemetery that spreads out and up a rolling hill from the back.

Dunia takes the stairs two at a time and holds the door open for her friend. They've arrived early and Ms. Zhanna Belovol, the choir director, is playing something on the piano. The girls sit down in the first pew and listen. This is something they haven't heard before. At first, the melody is light and lyrical and then it descends into something darker, filled with longing. Dunia feels it wrap its way around her. She closes her eyes. Her heart swells as the melody shifts. Then Zhanna begins to sing. The lyrics are part of a bible passage. Dunia knows this one. When Zhanna is finished, the girls applaud.

"What song is that?" Dunia asks, getting up from her seat and making her way around the piano.

"It's called *Do Not Fear*. I've been working on it all week," Zhanna replies.

"You wrote that?" Dunia says, her eyes scanning the pages of music.

"Tak," Zhanna says, smiling at Dunia.

"I want to write music like that," Dunia says, "Can we sing it now?"

One warm Sunday, a few weeks later, the villagers flow from their homes toward St. Vladimir's in the bright morning sunlight. The stream of parishioner's curve and wind their way up the path towards the massive double doors of the church. As the villagers merge, their greetings can be heard in harmony with the sounds of birds and a lone dog barking in the distance.

"Good morning," One woman says to another.

"And how's this little one?" the woman responds, reaching out to touch the cheek of a juicy baby resting in the arms of the first woman. The baby boy, just over a year old, is plump as a dumpling and smiling a toothy grin. His cheeks are shiny and red and he reaches out to grab a handful of the other woman's hair. She steps back and puts her hair over her shoulder.

"I know that move," she says to the baby and the mother at the same time. She has raised four of her own babies and managed to keep her long hair attached to her head. When the boy fusses at this, she continues to coo, "You can't have that, you can't have that." At this, the boy breaks into his toothy grin once again. Soon, he becomes distracted by the white fuzzy seeds floating in the air. The cottonwood poplars have released their fluff and it swirls in on the breeze, like snow. It gathers on the church steps and billows out again as the doors swing open and closed.

Dunia is already at church. She's been there for an hour, wringing her hands. The choir has been working on Zhanna's song for the past few weeks and today is its debut. Dunia has taken on the solo. She scans the congregation for her family. She waves when she sees them and settles back into the choir. The mass begins and Dunia's nerves ease as she relaxes into the flow of the service. After the homily, the choir sings. Dunia steps forward to sing her part.

"Even though I walk through the darkest
valley,
I will not be afraid, for you are close
beside me.
Your rod and your staff protect and
comfort me.
God is my shepherd He restores my soul;
He guides me in the paths of righteousness."

When Dunia sings, she is surprised by the sound of her own voice. She has a moment of recognition. 'That's my voice,' she thinks. It gives her courage and it also frightens her to be heard by everyone in this way. She closes her eyes and feels the power of the words, the beauty of the melody. She loses herself in the moment. And as quickly as it began, the song is over. It feels surreal, like waking up from a dream. Dunia returns fully to her feet and to the congregation. She steps back. She feels as if she has been sung - sung by something other than herself. When Dunia scans the congregation to connect with her mother, she sees that several of the parish-ioner's eyes are wet. 'What just happened?' she wonders.

As they walk the lane home, Dunia is still holding onto the experience with reverence. She walks next to her dad. Katya and Maroushka are still back at the church, wrapped up in conversations with a bustle of women near the church steps. Her brother, Krystian, is trailing behind them, whacking a stick into the bushes and scuffing his feet along the road, kicking up a cloud of dust. Dunia puts her hand in her father's hand and they walk together like that. They amble down the lane towards home, taking in the morning. Dunia notices the strength in her dad's hands and feels the calluses on his fingers. She sees how much darker the skin on his arm is, compared to hers. Several poplar seeds have attached themselves to the stubble on his chin. A fragrant breeze blows in from the river gently swaying the branches of the trees, back and forth, releasing a fresh cloud of fluff ahead of them on the road.

"You've got seeds on your chin," Dunia says, looking up at her father.

He runs his hand down his chin releasing the seeds to the wind. They share a smile and continue walking in reverie.

"It's not everything you know," Krystian says from behind them, breaking the spell.

"What do you mean?" Dunia says, looking back at him, surprised.

"Church, the choir, all that" he says, throwing a rock in the trees and gesturing back toward the church. "I'd rather be on the river any Sunday."

Dunia looks at him, confused.

"It's so boring and it doesn't mean anything," Krystian says, leaning in toward Dunia to emphasize his point and his size.

"That's enough!" Nepefan states, "If you want to go to the river, then go to the river. You don't have to spoil this Krystian. Just keep walking!" Dunia looks up at her dad. His brow is furrowed and he is looking at Krystian with a hard stare. Krystian stands there defiantly, staring back at his dad. Then he throws his stick into the trees and takes off down the road.

Dunia and Nepefan watch him go. About a quarter of a mile down the road, he looks back at them, kicks up the dirt and turns down a different path, in the direction of the river.

"Why did he say that?" Dunia asks.

Nepefan looks up at the leaves, shimmering in the breeze.

"I mean, he shouldn't say that about church, should he, Dad?" Dunia continues. "I guess he didn't like my song," she adds, dejectedly.

"No, it's not about you zychick[1]," her father begins, "Krystian is working something out for himself, but it's not about you. You mustn't think that it has anything to do with you. Your song was beautiful."

Dunia considers this.

"Ok?" he says. "You let Krystian be Krystian and you be you. Ok? He'll figure it out and he'll cool off by the river."

"Ok," Dunia responds, taking a breath.

---

1. rabbit

A finch sings a bright little song from the branches of a lilac bush. The light dapples down through the canopy of green hanging over the lane. Dunia smells apple blossoms and the cool freshness of the river on the breeze. Nepefan squeezes Dunia's hand. She looks up at him and squeezes back.

4

1913: LOVE

17 YEARS OLD

There's a young man in the village named Jacob. He's wild and beautiful, with dark eyes. His family moved here two years ago from a village north on the Voorskla River. They had cousins that lived in Kobelyiaky and decided to join farmsteads and put down new roots. They planted their fields with wheat and millet. They owned a horse, two cows, a cluck of chickens and a smattering of sheep.

Jacob runs around with Krystian and a band of unruly boys. They have been known to cause some trouble in the village; raiding gardens, drinking beer and brawling amongst themselves.

One night, the boys are having a fire near an old abandoned farmstead, shouting and howling at the moon, venting their energy. The night is mild, like bath water and a warm wind blows in from the east. A full moon hangs heavy in the sky and a feeling of electricity hangs in the air. The boys are wild. It's the kind of night that makes people do things they might later regret.

Krystian drags a massive gnarl of dead wood out of the forest.

"Throw it on the flames," one boy shouts.

"Yes, more wood," another one echoes, "Let's burn it all!"

Caught up in the madness of the evening, the boys keep adding more wood to the flames. Soon a bonfire blazes out of control and overtakes a dilapidated old shack that stands nearby. Once alight, there is nothing for the boys to do but watch in awe and horror as the shack burns sky high.

The flames draw a crowd and soon several men from the village are also among them, watching and shaking their heads as the old shack burns to the ground.

Luckily no one is hurt, but the next day punishment comes swiftly.

"You're going to be so busy, there won't be time for this kind of shit to happen," Jacob's father roars at him, "Ever again!" he adds, punctuating his words with a swift kick to Jacob's ass. The man is furious after hearing about the fire from a neighbor. He hadn't believed it to be true until he wandered down to the old farmstead himself, earlier that morning. The damage was breath-taking. Needless to say, the "posse" is disbanded for a time. Jacob is put to work on the farm. And truly, he has no time for anything else. He works, eats, sleeps and does it all over again every day for an entire month. His younger sister refers to the day of the bonfire as "Jacob's slightly charred incident." Jacob takes her taunts and endures his father's punishment with a measure of grace. In truth, the experience scared him and he's happy to cool his heels for a while.

One day, a few months later, when Jacob is free again, he walks through the front field in pursuit of his horse. Her name is Viter, which means wind. She's been named well because she's a wild thing. She goes where she pleases and nothing can hold her, except for the stable in winter, which Jacob decides is out of convenience and shy of the cold, more than anything else. Jacob can see Viter in the distance near the edge of a woods, head bent low, drinking from the brook. As he approaches he hears singing.

Dunia is in Zelenyy Lis foraging for herbs and greens- sorrel, purslane and wild mint line her basket. She's singing an old folk song. The tune is haunting and as Dunia sings, the hair on the back of her neck stands at attention. She can feel the pleasure of the song all the way down to her toes. This is one of her favorite places to be; in the woods, singing a song, her hands in the earth and the sun on her back. Jacob makes his way carefully to Viter and offers her a carrot, like a peace offering.

"I don't want to chase you all around Viter," he whispers, stroking the side of her neck. The horse gazes into the woods, looking for the source of the song. Jacob looks too and sees Dunia. She's down on the ground, gathering greens. Jacob watches her with curiosity. He knows Dunia as his friend Krystian's sister. Viter whinnies giving Jacob away. Dunia turns and looks at them.

"Hey there," she says, getting up from the ground. "How long have you been standing there?"

"I've been following my horse."

"Ah," says Dunia, making her way over. She looks beautiful and sun kissed, her hair is long and dark. Sveta braided it that morning, fashioning it into a crown around her head. Dunia tucked a sprig of little purple flowers behind her ear. Jacob looks at her. His cheeks are flushed.

"I'm gathering sorrel for our supper tonight. The borscht isn't the same without it," Dunia says, imitating her mother's voice and trying to act like an adult.

Jacob looks at her, nodding.

"Well, that's what my mother says anyways," Dunia explains, her cheeks flushing at the attention of this beautiful young man. "And the mint is for Maroushka, she uses it for tea," Dunia continues, nervous to be alone with this boy in the woods. "I love your horse," she continues, turning her attention to the animal.

Jacob pats Viter on the back, "She escaped twice in the last month," he says. "She just likes to be free, that's all."

Dunia knows who Jacob is and of the trouble he's gotten into with her brother. She doesn't approve of his behavior. All the same, she can't help but notice Jacob's strong hands, his broad chest and the chorded muscles in his arms.

"Where did you learn to sing like that?" Jacob asks her.

"Well, I've always sang, ever since I was a little girl but I'm also part of the church choir."

"Oh," he says. "I've never been to church before."

"Well, you should come!" Dunia says in a burst of excitement.

Jacob smiles, taking in the expression of naked exuberance on Dunia's face. Suddenly, Dunia feels shy and exposed. "I mean everyone should go to church you know," she says, twisting her hands together and trying to gain composure.

A few weeks later, Nepefan is standing around in the yard with some of his students. He has just finished a lesson and the kids are mingling about, gathering their things, scattering this way and that, or in the case of five year old student Olek, dancing around like a wild animal. Nepefan looks up and sees Jacob hanging back on the path, a tentative smile on his face. Jacob approaches and introduces himself. He mentions his interaction with Dunia in Zelenyy Lis and goes on to ask Nepefan for his permission to court Dunia.

Nepefan knows Jacob, as he knows everyone in the village. But this is their first formal introduction. Jacob is approaching Nepefan as a man, not a boy. Nepefan studies Jacob's face as he thinks for a moment. "You've been in some trouble recently," he says. It's not a question, more of an observation. Nepefan feels empathy, as his own son was involved in the fire too and he himself was a reckless young man once. But he doesn't give any of this away. He holds Jacob to his statement.

"Yes," Jacob says, "That was a crazy thing to do, a crazy mistake."

Nepefan nods, not letting him off the hook just yet.

"I worked hard for a month on the farm to make up for that. Nothing like that will ever happen again. I'm a good man. I know how to work a farm," he says, "I would take good care of your daughter."

Nepefan notices a bead of sweat that has collected on Jacob's forehead. Jacob wipes it away with the back of his hand.

"Well," Nepefan says, "I think you better ask Dunia."

Dunia hears their voices from inside the hut and comes out onto the porch.

"What's going on?" she asks, wiping her hands on her apron.

Jacob straightens up.

Dunia notices Jacob's size as he stands there next to her father. She's never seen the two men side by side and the experience is strange. She sees for the first time how big and broad Jacob is, at least a head taller than her father and Nepefan is not a small man."I'm just asking your Dad for permission to court you," he says nervously, unsure of what to do with his hands. "He said that I should ask you," he continues.

Dunia blushes and stands there, thinking for a moment, looking from Jacob to her Dad and then back again. She puts her hands on her hips and gives him a pointed look, "If you go to church, then yes," she replies.

The following Sunday Dunia is warming up her voice in the rectory of the church. She's thinking about Jacob and feels nervous as she moves out into the church and finds her place in the choir. She scans the congregation, looking for his face and there he is. Jacob has brought his mother, Daniela, and they sit five rows back with a clear view of the choir. He has combed his hair and put on clean clothes. His cheeks shine as he looks at Dunia. She exchanges a glance with Olena and tries to hide her excitement. But as usual, her red cheeks betray her.

After mass the two of them stand under an ancient oak and speak shyly.

"You came," Dunia says.

"The singing was the best part," Jacob responds, twisting his hat around in his hands.

Dunia blushes and laughs. She feels a landscape of feelings. She is proud of her voice and loves that Jacob was there to witness it. He is so beautiful and his presence makes her heart pound. She also feels embarrassed by her own excitement and nervousness. She always thought her older sisters acted silly around boys, and swore she would never do the same. But, here she is, blushing and twirling a long strand of her hair round and around her finger, powerless to be anything different than she is, in this moment.

Nepefan, Katya and Jacob's mother, Daniela, stand off to the side and chat, stealing the odd glance towards their children. It's awkward and exciting… filled with promise.

True to their agreement, Jacob attends church every Sunday and sits with Dunia's family among the rest of the parishioners. Sometimes his mother attends with him and although she isn't a religious woman, she's grateful to God for the influence Dunia is having on her wild son.

Jacob is confused by the traditions and the language of the mass. He struggles to make sense of what he hears in the readings and the sermon. There's no real connection there for him. But when the music plays and Dunia sings, the sanctity of the message is delivered with absolute clarity - like a bell rung directly from the heavens. For Jacob, Dunia's voice cuts through all the noise and chatter. It shines a light on him and more than once, Nepefan notices the light in Jacob's eyes as he listens to Dunia sing.

One day, after mass, Jacob heads home alone. His mother has stayed to chat with Katya but he's anxious to get out of his church clothes and spend time down by the river. The sky is blue with only a whisper of clouds and he wants to go fishing. As he wanders down the lane a few of his friends stand in a cluster, talking and casting the odd glance his way. They've noticed that Jacob attends church now and they know why too.

"Holy Jack," one of them calls out, teasing him,"your halo is blinding me!"

The boys make a game of shielding their eyes.

Jacob makes his way over to them, giving his friend a punch to the shoulder, laughing it off.

Jacob feels embarrassed by his friends' taunts, though he would never show it. He's used to acting tough and his recent actions run counter to his image. But something has shifted. It matters less to him, what his friends think. He wants to be with Dunia and the draw of that possibility has taken precedence. Jacob wants a wife, children, a family. He can see his future and it trumps the unfledged priorities of childhood.

5

1914: A WEDDING

Dunia and Jacob are married in the spring. The lilacs are in full blossom and the sweet fragrance billows through the open doors of St. Vladimir's Church. The sun shines through the stained glass windows reflecting warm yellow light on the faces of the villagers gathered there. The choir sings Zhanna Belovol's interpretation of a traditional wedding song. It's been slowed down and laced with harmonies. Jacob's Uncle Bohdan accompanies on the cello. Dunia and Jacob stand at the front of the church, before the priest, facing each other. Sveta has braided Dunia's hair and piled it up on her head with fresh flowers. Anichka, her oldest sister, traveled from her village in the south, in spite of her pregnancy. Fedir, who is still a mystery, moves and ripples underneath her belly. He responds to the music and in his mind, he is very much a part of the celebration.

After the ceremony, the family and the villagers mingle on the grass outside the church.

"I think we have another musician in the family," Anichka says, hand on her swollen belly. She's in her third trimester and her husband, Marko, stands close to her, hand on the small of her back, beaming. The two of them share a glow and, in her pregnancy, Marko has also put on weight.

"Is it the comfort of marriage?" Krystian asks, pointing to Marko's waistline.

"God, Krystian," Anichka responds, hitting him on the shoulder, "Do you ever think before you speak?"

"It's ok," Marko chimes in, "I wish you all the comforts of marriage one day. I think it would be the best thing for all of us…except for the bride of course. I pity her."

"Tak tak," Krystian replies with a laugh,"I deserve that."

"I guess I'm sharing the experience with my wife," Marko continues, taking Anichka's stance, one hand on his low back and the other resting on his belly.

Everybody laughs.

After a while, Dunia finds Jacob in the crowd and they stand facing each other, interlacing their fingers. Electricity passes between them and she can feel Jacob's heart pounding. Dunia understands the mechanics involved in consummating a marriage. She's aware of the intoxicating energy that she feels when she's around Jacob.

In the days leading up to the wedding, Anichka took Dunia aside and explained her version of what happened in a marriage bed. "It only hurts the first time," she says, "And there will be blood."

Dunia wrings her hands at this. She can't imagine doing something so intimate with someone. She can't imagine that her parents have done it. And Maroushka too! "I can't do it," Dunia says, "Do I have to?"

"Yes you can and yes you do," Anichka coos, "And trust me, you want to. After a while you might even like it." Dunia has never seen this side of her sister before. She feels equally drawn and repelled by her.

Dunia considers God in the equation. 'Will God be happy with me if I do it?' Dunia asks quietly, as she lies in bed one night. She tosses and turns, contemplating what is expected of her a few short days from now. 'Will God watch?' she asks herself, mortified at the thought. In the end, she concludes that sex is part of the divine plan. 'Ok God,' she prays, "I'm willing to participate in *that*.'

As Dunia stands in the shade of the tree, facing her husband - she sees the look in his eyes, intense and full of desire, a look she's never seen before. Now they're married and he has permission to look at her in this way. He puts his hand on her waist and gives it a squeeze. Dunia can't believe what's coming. She's breathless and wanting too.

The villagers disperse from St. Vladimir's and the family moves like a wave down main-street towards Jacob's family farm. Katya and Maroushka walk arm in arm discussing the layout of food and final preparations for the party. Daniela had gone ahead and the hustle and bustle is already underway in her family hut.

The women have been preparing food for days; borscht, varenyky[1], holubsti[2] and vinaigrette[3] all in various stages of completion cover the surfaces of the hut and the cooking area outside in the yard. There's a long table near an ancient hornbeam tree at the west end of the yard and it's draped in a red and white embroidered tablecloth. The center-piece is a golden, round braided bread called Korovai. The garden has been planted and is already teeming with buds and sprouts. Some of the sheep have given birth and fuzzy little lambs graze close to their mothers out in the field.

When the feast has been eaten and the dishes have been cleared, Nepefan pulls out his balalaika and begins to play a jaunty little tune. He is joined by another man on guitar and another playing a leather skin hand-drum. The tables are moved back to form a semi-circle around an open space that makes up the dance floor. The sun is lower on the horizon now, but still shines warm and bright on the yard. The blossoms from the chokecherry trees have scattered in the breeze and decorate the ground with delicate white petals. People make their way to the dance floor and start moving to the music. One man stands in the middle of the space teetering this way and that. He's drunk too much horilka and it shows in his wobbly dance moves. Maroushka watches the man, with a wry expression on her face and after a time, makes her way over to him and directs him to a bench, where he can rest his precarious legs and preserve his dignity.

1. sweet or savoury filled dumplings, commonly filled with potato and served with fried onions and sour cream.
2. Cabbage rolls –pickled cabbage wrapped around various fillings including meat, rice and seasoning.
3. a salad made from diced cooked and brined vegetables including beets, potatoes, onion and sauerkraut.

Children dart in and out, playing an impromptu game of tag, shouting and laughing, burning off the feast. Dunia dances in a circle with her sisters. She is radiant and bursting with joy. The women hold hands and move in towards each other, bringing their foreheads together, before moving out again. One little boy suddenly finds himself at the center of this circle. He stumbles in accidentally. A strategic move to avoid being tagged. Now the boy looks around shyly at the beautiful women as they dance in towards him. He has inadvertently become a participant in the dance and he's not sure how to escape and hasn't decided if he wants to yet.

Later, Jacob comes to claim a dance with his bride. He steps forward and takes Dunia by the hand. He leads her to the center of the dance floor. It's darker now. He inter-laces his fingers with hers and the two of them stand like this, looking at one another and swaying to the music. Dunia's heart pounds. She closes her eyes and presses her face into his chest, breathing in the scent of him. Her husband. Jacob rests his hands on Dunia's hips. The music continues, slow and melodic. The rhythm of the drum pulsing and holding a steady beat.

6

1918: FAMILY

Dunia helps Marta into her high chair and ties a fresh bib around her neck. Maroushka is sitting on a chair nearby, holding Katarina who is chewing contentedly on a soft towel. The kitchen has been cleaned up from breakfast and Marta's face is shiny from being wiped with a warm washcloth. She resisted her face wash, as she often does, but now she looks sweet as a plum once again. If you ask Marta how old she is, she'll proudly hold up three chubby little fingers. Right now, she is examining the fallen crumbs of her breakfast on the dirt floor of the hut. Dunia spreads flour across the counter and tips a big wooden bowl onto its side. A mass of sticky dough rolls out. She's preparing Paska[1] for Easter this coming Sunday. She cuts a small piece of dough off of the mass and puts it onto Marta's tray.

"Marta, watch here," Dunia says. She presses and kneads the dough with the heel of her hand. As the dough absorbs the

1. A sweet, golden bread served at Easter.

flour, she adds a new layer and finds her rhythm folding and pressing, turning and folding. It's like a dance. Marta watches her mother, with a serious expression on her face. Then she imitates, kneading and pressing her own piece of dough. After a while she tires of this. She brings the dough to her lips and takes a nibble.

"No Marta, don't eat that!" Dunia says, stepping forward and intercepting the *snack*, "this is just to play with," she says pointing at the dough. Marta gives Dunia a wounded look, her lip quivering. "I'll tell you what, once you've kneaded that piece of dough, we can bake it and then you can eat it with some butter. What do you think of that?" Dunia dusts the tray of Marta's high chair with flour. Marta seems to like that idea and she slaps at the dough flattening it into the tray. Her hand is covered in flour and she moves it across her face and into her hair leaving a white dusty trail.

"Paska," she says, trying out the word. She just heard it for the first time this morning and she's added it to her repertoire. "Paska paska paska," she repeats. " Yes, Paska," repeats Maroushka, who has been watching with an amused expression on her face, "You say that so well, my darling."

Marta has started "talking" to Katerina, speaking the words she knows and trying to string sentences together. Sometimes Katerina will respond to Marta's chatter with a coo or a series of gurgles. They'll go back and forth like this, having a little "conversation." Marta can communicate most of what she needs- bread, cheese, juice, up, tired and of course, "no!"

Dunia kneads the dough until it's smooth and round as a baby's bum. Then she puts it back in the bowl. She stops for a moment to breathe in the fragrance of the dough. This is one of Dunia's favorite smells- the yeast, the sweetness, the tang of fermentation. The smell brings back a memory of making Paska with Mamo and Baba when she was just a little girl. Her mother showed her how to turn the extra dough into little baby chicks called Kurchata, using cloves for eyes and flaring out the little tail with three careful slices of the knife. This is the first year she's been organized enough to make Paska since having Marta. She drapes a piece of cloth over the bowl and sets it near the oven to rise.

"Do you want some tea?" she asks. Maroushka is gently rocking Katarina now and humming a tune. The baby stares up at a ray of sunlight dancing back and forth on the ceiling. Her slow blinks tell Dunia that sleep is imminent. Maroushka nods, not wanting to pull Katarina from her reverie.

"Chamomile?"

"Tak."

Maroushka was up at the crack of dawn this morning, as she is most mornings; taking care of the garden, sweeping up the yard, planning meals, tending sheep and foraging for herbs and berries. She enjoys the simple pleasure of her routine. This is trumped only by visits with her great-grand-children.

Anichka and Krystyan are both married and living in neighboring villages; Anichka to the south and Krystyan to the north. It's harder for Maroushka to close these distances but she, Nepefan and Katya took the trip earlier this spring to see Anichka's new baby and Fedir, who's four now. Fedir is slower than Marta to speak and form sentences. He gets frustrated trying to be understood. He pounds his little fists on the ground, or throws his head back in the air and wails. He's easy to love, even in his difficulty.

Nikolai and Sveta have both set up their homes on the family land, sharing the responsibility of tending to the animals and sharing meals. Nepefan, Jacob and the boys worked together to build separate huts with piche ovens of their own. Over the years the garden has expanded, doubling in size and growing a big crooked arm in the direction of Sveta's hut. Nikolai and Sveta both acquired more animals in their marriages- sheep, chickens and a few cows and these effects became part of the family's resources. Everything is shared between them. The farm is an abundant and simple place.

Maroushka walks the distance from her place on the farm to Dunia and Jacob's hut. Even in the dead of winter, Maroushka puts on her boots and ventures into the cold for a chance to relax with a cup of tea and a chubby baby in her arms. In the winter, she arrives at the door, a big indistinct bundle. She appears as a set of eyes decorated with white frosty eyelashes, the rest of her hidden under a mass of clothing; parka, scarf, boots, hat and mitts.

Now, Maroushka leans in to smell Katerina's sleepy little head. She kisses her cheek and smooths out her hair. Katerina has a shock of blond hair, whereas Marta has dark hair and dark eyes like her mother. Dunia is amazed by their difference in personality. Marta is fiery and stubborn and Katerina is easy and relaxed. The balance works. It's a blessing to have such an easy baby after her first few years of motherhood. Marta's nature expanded the limits of Dunia's patience beyond what she thought possible. The challenge of their relationship and Marta's unending need brought Dunia to her knees on more than one occasion.

"Nothing will grow you up faster than raising a child," her mother had often said. She was there for Dunia in her most difficult times, spelling her off and giving her a chance to rest, while Jacob was out working the land and providing for the family.

Dunia knows that she is with child again. She felt it for the first time a few weeks ago, the sensation of tiny bubbles traveling through her belly and a week later a more distinct feeling, like the fluttering of a butterfly wing.

7

1918: POLITICAL UNREST

Dunia stokes the fire and moves her chair closer to Jacob and away from the curling smoke. The babies are asleep, tucked into their beds like little buns. The sky is luminous with stars and a waxing crescent moon. Dunia's pregnancy is showing now – she, her own waxing crescent moon. Jacob puts his arm around her and kisses the side of her head. He spent the day with Nepefan and Krystian smoking pork sausage in the yard.

"You smell like garlic," Dunia says, leaning into her husband.

"And you smell like the wind," he replies, breathing in the scent of her hair.

Krystian and his wife, Alyona, came down from their village in the North bringing wild garlic and cloves to season the meat and an embroidered shawl for each of the women.

"They're staying at Sveta's tonight?" Dunia asks.

"Yes, they're packed in tight over there."

Dunia smiles, thinking about the hut she grew up in, with every spot and surface occupied by sleeping family members. The evening is mild and a gentle breeze whispers through the field. Jacob watches the grass as it sways back and forth. Viter, their horse, whinnies from somewhere behind the hut. Jacob looks toward the sounds, anticipating more noise from the animal. When there is none, he settles down again by the fire. "She's been restless," he says, gesturing in Viter's direction.

Dunia and Jacob look into the fire, admiring the glow of the embers and the flames licking up into the darkness.

Jacob speaks, "If Krystian didn't have a family here, he would be in Kiev, fighting."

"What did he say?" Dunia asks, turning toward her husband.

"That Skoropadsky[1] and his new government are a disgrace, that they're undoing everything the Central Rada[2] set out to do."

"Nikolai was over here the other day and he was saying something similar, he was writing an article about it for his newspaper."

"He's angry, Dunia; he's so angry, I've never seen him like that and this is Krystian we're talking about."

---

1. General Pavlo Skoropadsky – An aristocratic, military leader that overthrew the Central Rada, handing power and control of Ukraine to the Austrian and German governments.
2. An all Ukrainian parliamentary government that declared independence for Ukraine, passing laws protecting minorities and uniting soldiers, peasants and workers in an attempt to create autonomy for the Ukrainian people.

Dunia wrings her hands and thinks about her brother, she's seen his anger on display more than once and she wonders exactly what he's capable of. "What's he going to do?" she asks.

"I don't know but people want to fight back."

"Yes, I know."

"I can't believe this is happening," Jacob says, reaching down to pick up a fresh log and place it in the fire. "We were just starting to get a taste of our independence and now they're taking it all away."

"Yes, they weren't in power for very long, were they."

"From April to January – nine months."

"Nine months," Dunia repeats thoughtfully, putting her hand on her swollen belly. "Do you think they'll reorganize?"

"They already are."

"I know that too." Dunia says, releasing a puff of air and leaning in to stir the fire with a charred stick. "I ask, but I already know," she says, exasperated. The wind picks up for a moment, causing the trees to bend and sway, fanning the flames. The fire crackles and pops and Dunia takes a step back to avoid a burst of hot embers. "And I don't want to know, at the same time," she says, sitting down next to Jacob once again. "Nikolai was telling me about it earlier this week. He was talking about farmers and peasants gathering in groups, organizing around the dinner table and out in the fields, creating their own armies."

"We all want to be free."

"I know, I know. Believe me, that's what I want too. I want that for our children," Dunia says, "Those girls, she says, gesturing towards the hut, tears welling up in her eyes. "They're everything! We need to protect them." Dunia sits back and stares out into the darkness of the field and the shadow of the forest beyond. "But I just worry about what it will cost," she says finally, taking Jacob's hand in hers and pressing her lips to his knuckles. She squeezes her eyes shut and tears drip down her cheeks. Jacob leans in and wraps his arms around Dunia, "The Central Rada was doing such good work," she says, "Why did it have to end?"

"Krystian says that they're organizing a new political party."

"Well, he'll want to be right in the middle of it - and Nikolai too!" she says, wrapping her shawl more tightly around her shoulders. The conversation settles and together they stare into the fire. Dunia is hypnotized by the movement of the flames and the red hot glow of the embers.

Later that night she sits on her chair by the oven and nurses Katerina. She can see Marta sleeping in her bed, arms thrown up in total surrender. She can't stop thinking about the political unrest. She feels threatened. She feels powerless over everything; the politics, the government, her brothers, her husband and even her own children. The political trajectory feels imminent. Like a vicious monster has been released in Kiev and is now tracking them, slowly making its way to their door. 'It looks totally peaceful from inside this hut,' she thinks, pausing again to look at Marta's beautiful face. She feels a contraction in her heart. It makes its way up into her throat and wraps its way around her head. She looks down at Katerina nursing at her breast and the feeling breaks. Dunia weeps. She weeps for her babies and for all of the babies being born into her family, at this time, with all the dangers of the outside world. The tears drip down her face and splash onto Katerina's head. For a moment Katarina opens her eyes and looks up at her mother, Dunia's nipple still held fast in her mouth. Mother and daughter look at each other like that. Katerina watches her mother's face with the complete openness and curiosity of a child. 'It's like looking at God,' Dunia thinks, pausing her emotion to bask in the beauty of her baby looking back up at her. After a time, Katerina closes her eyes again and goes back to nursing peacefully. Dunia is gripped by grief. It wracks her body and turns her inside out. All the while, Katerina sucks and slurps in the absolute security of her mother's arms.

8

1918: HARVEST

It's early morning and Dunia stands in her garden barefoot, gazing out toward the field in the distance. A mist has threaded and curled its way around the stooks decorating the landscape. At first glance, in the darkness and the mist, they look like shaggy beasts. They've been drying and curing there over the past two weeks in preparation for threshing. The village has one thresher that farmers share, taking turns and working together to complete the harvest. Today, it's their turn, and soon the farm will be bustling with men in the fields working the thresher with sweat and muscle. The kitchen will brim too, with women chatting and laughing as they chop, peel and mix to prepare the meals required to feed the hungry crew.

Now, the sun is coming in sideways through the trees on the horizon, illuminating the golden wheat. The morning is cool but Dunia is hot with her pregnancy and enjoys the feeling of the moist black earth on her feet and toes. A cow lows gently from its shed, a plea for sweet relief. The sound pulls

Dunia from her reverie and forward into her day's work. She traces her way back to the hut through carefully laid rows, admiring the vegetables and greens of her garden. Dunia slides her feet into her wooden clogs, removes the cream pail from its nail on the back side of the hut and makes her way across the yard to the cow shed.

Dunia bends low and takes her seat on the milking stool. Sophie grunts and shuffles her feet in anticipation.

"Ok, I know," Dunia coos, putting a warm hand on Sophie's flank and giving her a gentle rub. She really does *know* how it feels.

When Dunia returns to the hut, Marta is awake, sleepy eyed and perched at the side of Katerina's basket watching her stretch and wriggle her way out of the blankets. Dunia puts the cream on the counter, kisses Marta on her fuzzy head and scoops up the warm little bundle. She settles herself by the empty hearth to feed her baby.

Soon, Jacob emerges from their bedroom, fully dressed. He's washed his face and neck and his cheeks have a shine to them. He's brown from the summer and his labor in the fields. This is his favorite time of year and he's expecting the sound of the thresher up the lane at any moment. He puts his hands on Dunia's shoulders and buries his head in the back of her neck.

"It's going to be hot," she says.

"Hmmm," he breathes into her hair.

"I'm going to feed you before you go out."

"Okay."

Jacob is consumed by his work at this time and has been known to miss a meal, just completely forget to eat, his hunger trumped by the pleasure and urgency of the harvest. There's a lot to do and a limited amount of time to do it in, with the impending press of winter and first frost, which isn't far off now. He and the men from the village will work today from sun up to sun down to stay ahead of it.

"Can you light the stove in the summer kitchen?" she asks, absorbed in her task.

"Yeah," Jacob releases her with a kiss to the cheek.

Katerina is done with her breakfast now and she twists and turns toward Marta who is playing a gourd rattle and singing a little song, partly for her own pleasure and partly to gain the attention of her mother.

Dunia recognizes the tune and sings along with Marta. It's a folk song about a little mosquito on his wedding day and Marta learned it, this past winter, from Nepefan, who sang it by the hearth, accompanied by his balalaika. Once Marta heard it for the first time, she kept asking to hear it again and again until the family was thoroughly saturated with it. Dunia had finally explained to Marta that "Didoo," Marta's name for her Grandpa, had to put his balalaika away now because *it* was tired.

Katerina turns back to her mother now, concentrating on her face and watching her lips as she sings.

Dunia holds up her baby and kisses her velvety cheek, breathing in her delicious scent. Next, she expertly ties Katerina to her body with a long wrap-around shawl and taking Marta's hand, leads her out to the summer kitchen which is separate from the hut and open to the elements.

Breakfast is millet porridge - harvested from their fields - with fresh cream, stewed apples and honey. Dunia also prepares an omelet made with fresh mushrooms foraged from the east forest and seasoned with salt and wild sage. Marta rolls a stump that she claimed as her step-stool last summer, toward the counter so she can watch Dunia cracking eggs and chopping herbs. Marta helps by stirring the eggs. Her favorite part is when the mixture lands in the hot pan and bubbles. She always plugs her ears anticipating the dramatic sizzling sound. Dunia smiles at Marta's innocent tenderness. The little family gathers outside to eat at the long table near the garden.

After a while, a mechanical rumble and chug of the thresher can be heard in the distance. Jacob finishes his last bite, kisses his wife and ducks into the hut for a moment. He emerges wearing his hat and heads off down the lane to greet the men of the village - Krystian and Nikolai are among them. The thresher has come into view now, a 20-ton steam engine slowly parading its way up the lane. It's followed by a group of men and older boys, vibrating with anticipation. Harvest time marks their transition from boys to men and the pride and excitement shows on their faces. There are a few younger boys in the crowd too, and they have the important job of bringing water to the men as they work in the fields.

The women appear next from around the bend in the lane. Maroushka, Katya, Sveta and several other women from the village are arriving with various ingredients for the day's meals. They carry baskets with beets and greens from their gardens, fresh eggs and jars filled with various pickles and preserves. Some of the women carry babies wrapped tightly to them with long pieces of fabric. There are also several children in tow, two of them close to Marta's age.

Marta stands in the garden sucking her fingers, watching the procession, transfixed and slightly terrified by the noise. The thresher releases a cloud of black smoke and announces itself with a shrill whistle. It veers off to the left and takes its place in the field near the first row of stooks. The men follow and gather in the field. Several are carrying pitchforks. They are poised and ready to begin. One man spears a stook and tosses it into the thresher. The other spread out, following suit. They've done this before and it won't take them long to find their rhythm. The women continue up the lane towards the garden and the hut and soon their voices and chatter can be heard above the mechanical din. Dunia greets them warmly. Hugs and kisses are exchanged and "oohs" and "ahhs" about the children who are "growing up so fast."

Maroushka disentangles Katerina from Dunia and joyfully assumes the first shift of caring for the children. The rest of the gaggle then makes its way to the summer kitchen and sets to work on lunch. The women descend on the space like bees on a field of clover and before long there is a buzz of activity, chopping and mincing, stirring and mixing, flouring and kneading and all to the tune of their voices and laughter. For women, the kitchen is a social place where stories are exchanged and bonds are formed over labor shared.

"So I was heating up the fat in the oven, like you told me to," says Sava, a young mother from the village. She is speaking to Vila, one of her neighbors. "But I guess I must have let it get too hot, because it caught on fire and the whole hut filled up with smoke."

"Oh no," Vila replies, a concerned expression creasing her brow. Vila was chopping carrots, but stops mid-chop to take in her friend's story.

"Well, the girls got on their coats and went out into the yard to escape the smoke and flames."

Now, all of the women are quiet, listening to Sava's story.

"Anyways, the next day, I thought I would give it another try, so I took the second lump of fat and started to prepare it the same way that I did the first time, making sure the oven wasn't quite as hot as the day before. My daughter says to me, in her bossy little voice, 'You're making it again?' And when I told her that I was, she gathered her sister and the two of them immediately put on their coats and left the house to go spend the afternoon in the yard."

At this, the women erupt into laughter.

The piche oven is hot now and Dunia wipes a bead of sweat from her forehead. The day rolls on like this with breaks only for lunch and supper which is finally served after the sun has gone down. By that time, Marta is falling asleep in her high-chair and Maroushka, who is also exhausted, scoops her up and takes her into the hut.

After a time, Dunia follows, to find them both spooned up together, fast asleep in Marta's bed. She covers them with a soft sheet and returns to the long table where Jacob and a few men are still gathered, talking by torch light. She clears up a few remaining plates and dishes and joins her mother, Sveta and Alyona, who are sitting nearby, finishing a cup of tea and warming themselves by the hot embers still aglow in the fire-pit. The conversation has heated up too and she can hear Krystian venting his rage about the political situation around Kiev.

"Those Bolshevik bastards are trying to take what isn't theirs to take. They think they can come here and rip the government right out of our hands and take the bread right out of our mouths and our children's mouths."

There's a part of Dunia that doesn't want to hear about it, doesn't want to know that this is happening. Village life here hasn't been affected yet but the boundaries of the violence are broadening and expanding, licking outwards like flames towards Kobelyiaky.

"I want to fight," Krystian says. "They're helping themselves to our country saying that we shouldn't take up space or even exist; that our culture is nothing. Next they'll be telling us to speak their language."

Dunia doesn't want Jacob to hear the rawness of Krystian's expression. She knows that he has a fire burning for the cause too. Everyone has been infected by the injustice of what's happening, but she's terrified that he will get involved. She's terrified of losing him. The rebellion in the summer was a bloody defeat and she wants to keep him out of it.

Nikolai speaks up "These forced food requisitions and land theft are enraging citizens and sparking violent rebellion all over the place." He throws a stick into the fire angrily. Everyone is quiet, focused on Nikolai, who has a keen interest in the press, and a unique view of what's been going on. He continues, empowered by the attention, "The enemy steals our resources and grain to feed *their* war effort. They haven't been able to shut down the free press yet but that could be next. They know we're more vulnerable if we don't have a clear picture of what's going on and it makes it more difficult for us to organize."

"But we need to fight back!" Krystian shouts, unable to restrain himself.

Nikolai continues without pause, "There are partisan groups springing up all over the place, men, farmers, peasants gathering and organizing to fight. The Ukrainian National Union has been formed now in response to Bolshevik forces and the Hetman government and they want our support in fighting back."

"It's the only thing to do," Krystian says, "We have wives, we have children, we have this land, this farm. We can't sit back and let them take it."

Dunia and Alyona exchange glances. The embers pop and crackle. Dunia stirs the coals with a stick, conjuring up a flame. Stars illuminate the night sky and a wolf howls in the distance.

9

1918: WINTER

The political turbulence rages on and by late October, Krystian and a group of men set off from the village to join the battle. The early morning light casts long shadows out in front of them as they march down the road that leads on to Dnepropetrovsk. They are laden with warm clothing and provisions for the journey- heavy jackets, scarves, woolen mittens and fur hats to protect their sweet heads. Back-packs and satchels sag with the weight of meals packed and prepared by the loving hands of wives, mothers, sisters and grandmothers. These women are left holding the weight of their unmeasured losses and the desperate hope that each man returns home safely and soon. From Dnepropetrovsk, the men will catch a train to Kiev, straight into the bloody heart of the conflict.

The villagers of Kobelyiaky gather to give them a proper send off, calling out to them, the women waving their scarves. The composed reverie gives way to reverence as they watch their men shrink into the distance; beautiful boys that grew up running around the village and making mud pies along the Kobeliaky River, headed out now, to face God knows what. Alyona, Krystian's wife, stands pale faced in their wake, clutching her shawl to her chest watching them disappear around the bend in the lane. When they are gone from sight, the spell is broken. The villagers move this way and that, chatting softly and returning to the tasks of the day. Life goes on. There are still cows to milk and children to feed.

Only Alyona is left staring at the empty lane for a long time. A thick fog wraps itself around her and the sounds of the village become muffled and distant. She can't seem to grasp the next thing that she's meant to do. The possibility that Krystian may never return, settles like an icy fist in her gut. His rage at the injustice of the political crisis has been consuming him for months. Alyona knew this day was coming. She had watched his eyes go dark and his patience grow thin and taut. He would miss meals and spend the evenings gathered around the bahattya[1] with the other men, exchanging information and pouring fuel on his own convictions. She wanted to slow him down. She wanted to pull him back home. But word of the conflict arrived almost daily to stoke his fury. By the time the group of men decided to leave, Krystian was smoldering for the cause and there was nothing for her to do but get out of his way.

Alyona is a gentle creature, her fragility a foil to his ferocity. In the end she swallowed her words and gave way to his need to engage in the battle. In his mind, he was already at war and would not be stopped. She sobbed quietly that

1. Bon-fire.

morning as she packed a haversack with smoked sausage, cheese, apples and several hard loaves of bread.

"I'm sorry," he said as she wrapped a scarf around his neck and kissed him a salty goodbye.

"I'll see you again soon okay?"

Alyona lingers on her last words to him, praying that they are not truly her last. Katya, terrified for her son, says nothing and leads Alyona back into her hut. She's invited Alyona to stay with her and Nepefan for a few days, afraid of what it might be like for her to face her grief alone.

Civilian bands of men swarm from every region of the country. It's as if they're driven by instinct, like worker bees to a hive. They've been called to face the Bolsheviks, the Red Army and the madness of war. They aren't trained soldiers with guns and uniforms. They're insurgent armies of peasants, farmers, Kulaks[2], fathers, brothers and sons defending their country with passion and pitchforks. They join forces with Ukrainian military operations already mobilized near the capital. Together they make headway against the enemy and Ukrainian forces occupy the city of Lviv on November 1st. The victory is sweet but bitterly short. The Polish army overtakes them and seizes the city on November 21st. In the days that follow, the tug of war over land and resources continues with Russian, Polish, German and Austrian forces stepping in at various times to stake their claim on Ukrainian territories. Kiev changes hands regularly with one authority giving way to the next. Each new governor brings

---

2. Prosperous peasants that owned land and could afford to hire workers

new rules, land boundaries, agendas, priorities and a new propagation of right and wrong.

That winter, the village holds vigil. All eyes are on the road that leads to Dnepropetrovsk. The villagers are hungry for news from the capital and word from their men. Dunia bundles up and walks to St. Vladimir's twice a week with Katerina strapped to her chest and Marta in tow. They spend time with her community. The parishioners pack into the pews, shoulder to shoulder, supporting one another and staving off the cold. After an hour or so the collection of bodies and the glowing beeswax candles warm the space to the point that Marta is shedding her scarf and woolen mittens and looking around for someone to play with. A small group of children gather in the back of the church. There is an old wooden box with a growing collection of picture books and hand-made toys. The children entertain themselves and mothers take turns tempering the children's exuberance so the adults can pray. Dunia prays for the safe return of her brother and the other village men- praying for them to have the strength to defeat the enemy and stay alive. When the candles have reached the end of their wick, parents re-bundle their children and head out of the smoky church and down the snowy lane in different directions toward home. Finally free of the need to play quietly, Marta throws handfuls of snow into the air, squealing as it floats back down landing in her hair and decorating her eyelashes. Katerina's cheeks are round and rosy as apples and her eyes glitter as she watches Marta's antics. She giggles at the sight. Dunia kisses her baby, smelling the sweetness of her child and beeswax candle smoke in her hair. Marta then decides that she wants to roll home and Dunia trails her circuitous "footprint" for a while.

Jacob had wanted to go to Kiev. He wanted to be on that train, but in the end, refused to leave Dunia who is round and heavy. By mid-February, Dunia is so big and swollen, she can hardly make the trip down the lane. This pregnancy is different from the two before and she's retaining so much fluid it worries her. As Jacob helps her into her winter boots, his finger leaves an impression in her skin that remains there for a few moments. It's not painful but strange. The midwife assures her that all is well and to continue drinking water and sipping on peppermint tea throughout the day. Her puffy skin becomes a novelty between her and Jacob. He jokes that the neighbors will see his intentions on her finger-printed skin.

Marta has already taken full ownership of the "new baby." She doesn't understand where the men have gone, but she understands that soon she'll have a new baby brother or sister. She has embraced the role of big sister with a jubilance that has her nesting right alongside of Dunia. They spend the morning cooking and baking, preparing the house for the baby.

"You are such a help," Dunia says to a beaming Marta.

When Dunia brings out Marta's old bassinet, now intended for the baby, Marta takes her stuffed bunny, Moony, and tries to lay once again in the little cradle. The bed is dwarfed by her size. She manages to lay down head to bum but her arms and legs are spilling out of the sides and she has to steady herself with her feet so as not to tip the whole thing over. When Dunia witnesses the sight and Marta's quivering lip, she has to turn away to hide her mirth. It's Marta's howl and tears that bring her back. "That was mine," Marta wails, "I'm not a baby anymore."

Later that day, when Maroushka arrives for a visit, Marta answers the door with Moony tucked under her shirt exclaiming "I'm having a baby!"

They spend the afternoon baking Pampushka[3] stuffed with fruit preserves and cottage cheese and Dunia stands with both hands on her belly declaring, "Tsya bulochka zakinchena!"[4]

That evening, she gazes out the kitchen window as the sun, low and bright in the sky, catches a dusting of intricate snow crystals decorating the ash tree outside her window. She is surprised by a warm rush down her legs and looks down to see a pool of liquid at her feet. The war doesn't have the power to hold life back. Dunia has no more time to consider the fate of the village men. She has a battle of her own. She puts the kettle on the stove in between contractions as Jacob runs through a thick carpet of snow and down into the village for the midwife. In spite of the war, the battle, the rage, the injustice - life in the village goes on and Dunia is about to shed her own blood to bring another life into the world.

---

3. Small yeasted buns
4. This bun is done

Years go by
Life continues
So does death.
Dunia gives birth to a son – Ivan.
Over the next few years, some of the men return to the village, and others do not.
Those that return are not the same.
There are injuries; visible and invisible.
The war carries on in the capital and beyond, raging overtly, like a rabid animal.
Then dipping down to almost nothing,
Leading the people to question.
"Is it over? Are we safe now? Can we go on living in peace?"
But the war beat is still drumming. Still pulsing steadily below the surface.
Bubbling in a covert fury – blood and tar, flames and darkness.
Time passes in Kobeliaky.
The family grows.
Six winters come and go.
Dunia has given birth now to three sons –
Ivan, Andrei and Alex.

10

1925: IVAN

(IN HIS OWN VOICE)

Mamo[1] is teaching me how to read. I thought that reading was singing cause that's how Mamo does it. She sing from the Bible with her sing-songy voice. Every night she sing before bed-time with me. She holds Alex in the rocking chair that Papa builded. The rest of us kids are snuggled up. Mamo says we're her little snuggle buns. I share my bed with Andrei. And Marta shares with Kat. Alex always falls asleep first. I'm not tired. My eyes just want to go to sleep but I am *not* tired! Then it gets real dark and quiet outside. Plus Mamo's voice singing and Papa by the fire. Crackle, crackle and the light moving around on the wall.

At my school, Didus[2] asked me to read in front of everyone. I stand and sang it just like Mamo do. I sang

The dog walks down the path
He follows his nose

1. Mom
2. Grandpa

The other kids laughed at me. I didn't get to finish. Why did they do that? I felt really shy after that time. I was hiding my face and didn't want to come out again. I'm a sad little turtle. I don't want to read any more ever again! Didus came over and squeezed my hand like that. That was nice. Didus is nice to me and he never laughed with the other kids. Then he taught us all a song about a big gray cat and his bowl of milk. I cannot stop singing that song sometimes!

Me and Symon were playing cats at school after that time. At home I'm going to be a cat for a while. Mamo gave me a bowl of milk. She put it on the floor and I crawled around like that. I want to eat it up just like Sasha do -with a little bit of milk on her tongue every time; Niav Niav[3]. Her tongue is so scratchy. Like a scratchy little comb. Sasha is a very licky cat but she's nice. She lives in a barn. Did you know that? I wanted to live out there with her one time but Papa said no. I wanted to sleep in the hay and worm down into it like a little mouse. I'm not scared of that but I think Papa thought I was. One time there was a hooty owl that lived out there. It had a baby owl too. Papa showed me its fuzzy little face poking down. We had to be real quiet that time. I just said "hu hu[4]," very quietly. Oh, and about before, I never got to finish my milk. Alex put his hand right into it. He spilled *my* milk everywhere. He's such a baby.

I'm six years old now and that's bigger than I've ever been! I'm bigger than Andrei and way bigger than Alex cause he's just a baby. He cries all the time and Baba says you can never take your eyes off him when he's so little. I think it's cause

3. Meow Meow
4. Hoot Hoot

she thinks he's really cute. And maybe cause he might crawl away if she's not looking. He could roll in the fire or hurt himself very badly. Baba says we all have to take good care of him. I love Alex but sometimes I cover my ears or go outside when he cries so much. Plus he always fall down, get up, fall down, get up and trying to walk some more. He should see me. I can run! I'm fast like *zoooooooom*!!

Dyad'ko[5] Krys (Krystian) can't run anymore. He can only walk with a crutch. He's very slow and grumpy sometimes. Papa says we need to be quiet when he comes over. Mostly they sit by the bahattya[6] and talk about stuff. I want them to play with me but mostly I play with Marta and Kat. We play in the back field. They always want to play house and I have to be the papa or the sobaka[7]. That's ok I guess. Mamo says Dyad'ko's leg was hurt very badly when he went to Kiev. She's sad about it sometimes. I saw her cry that time. I never want to go there. I need my legs to run fast! He keeps his leg wrapped up all the time. But I saw it once. He took off his bandage when Papa was there. I was sneaking a look from behind a tree. Then I saw it up close. Papa said it was ok. I was covering my face and peeking through my fingers. It looked all red and messy. Like something tried to chew his leg up. I saw one part that was sown (sewed) up tight. Did you know you could sew someone up? I didn't want to look ever again after that time. But I think now I want to see it again next time. Is that bad?

5. Uncle
6. Bon-fire
7. Dog

We're going to the forest today to play. Baba's taking us there- me and Marta and Kat but not Andrei and not the baby. He's too loud for that. Plus he's always crying and squirming around everywhere. He'll scare all the fish away. I'm going to look for fish in the brook. They live there. Did you know that? I wonder where they go when it's frozen? I think about that sometimes.

I'm taking Papa's net. I'm going to feed them some of my bread but don't tell Mamo. She says that bread's for me. But those fish are so hungry sometimes. Papa said there was a big brown bear that lived in the forest. I think it's living in a dark cave somewhere. I want to find that cave and spy on that bear. I bet he'd be snoring loudly or maybe eating something up. Like a sheep or a chicken. Do bears like fish? Baba says they do. But we can't get close to bears! Baba says they're too grumpy sometimes. I always carry a big sharp stick when I go to the forest. I'll scare that bear back into his cave for good.

My Baba knows the forest better than anyone. She was a little girl in that forest once. She showed my where all the berries growed. Today we're going to pick blueberries. Baba says they're ready to eat. I help pick blueberries but I can never save any. I eat them up like that. Kat says I have purple lips and a purple tongue. Those are my most favorite ones ever! Baba bakes treats for us sometimes. She puts some of them in jars too. I know how good they are cause we ate them for dessert sometimes when dyad'ko and titon'ka [8] come over for supper.

8. Auntie

11

1928: POLITICAL SHIFT

Nepephan and Katya's farm has burst open in celebration despite a dark, looming political agenda. There are four September birthdays in the family; Nikolai, Mykhailo, Sveta's daughter Helena and Maroushka. The feast has already been devoured. A few people are still lingering around the big wooden table, nibbling on this and that. A wrinkled old man with a long beard and a wizened face is nodding off in the shade of the massive oak tree. He is Stepan, the oldest man in the village. The summer is still hanging on. The heat of the afternoon sun is ripening the watermelons in the field and the apples in the orchard. The stems and branches bend and sway under the weight of their fruit.

Krystian and Alyona are making their way up the lane and Nikolai runs out to greet them.

"We are only just here," Alyona says apologetically, "the cake took longer to bake this time."

"Ho brother! Alyona, welcome," Nikolai says, acknowledging the honey cake she's brought for dessert while simultaneously relieving her of a bottle of horilka[1]. There's an old Baba that runs a distillery out of her potato farm south of Kobelyiaky. Alyona trades her renowned baking for a bottle or two.

"Nobody's Horilka is as clear as mine," the Baba says proudly, whenever Alyona shows up with an armload of goodies.

Alyona clasps Nikolai in a hug before scurrying off towards the festivities with her offering.

"Four decades old man," Krystian says, embracing his brother, "Happy Birthday!"

"There's no one to grumble about all the noise because we've invited the whole village!" Nikolai says, gesturing to the hearty crowd. The men laugh at the old family joke. Krystian takes a deep breath and leans on his crutch, a weary expression showing through the smile on his face.

The men move toward the oak tree and sit down on a massive log. Krystian sets his crutches down and winces as he tries to find a comfortable position for his leg. Nikolai looks out at the yard and cracks open the bottle of booze. He leans back and takes a swig. He holds it in his mouth for a moment and then swallows. Then he examines the bottle in his hands and breathes in sharply, "She really knows what she's doing," he says, handing the bottle over to Krystian. "We all know what's coming," Nikolai says dryly, "and yet here we are celebrating anyway."

1. Hard liquor or spirit, like vodka

"I'm sure Maroushka had a hand in that," Krystian responds, knowingly.

"They all did. We might as well make merry and eat everything we have before they rip it out of our hands," Nikolai says, reaching into his pocket and pulling out a deeply creased article from the Ukrainski Holoc[2]. He flattens it out against his thigh and presents it to Krystian.

The free press has been a slow burning passion and pride for Nikolai since the first world-war. He began corresponding with the editor three years ago. They had been sharing thoughts and ideas for a time and that connection developed into a job last year. Nikolai submits articles regularly. He keeps a steady finger on the political pulse of the country. It enlivens him and destroys him equally.

"By this time next month this farm may not belong to us anymore," he continues as Krystian studies the article. The sunlight filters through the swaying forest trees behind them, casting dappled light onto the paper. Krystian's brow creases and knits as he absorbs his brother's words.

"How is this happening?" Krystian asks, finally, handing the article back to Nikolai and propping his mangled foot onto a wide rotten stump, decorated with patches of orange and green lichen. "I feel so helpless now," he says, looking defeated.

Nikolai neatly folds the article and returns it to his pocket, smoothing the fabric of his pants. "Last week a group of Soviet officials came here, you know. They were taking stock

2. Ukrainian Voice (A nationalist newspaper)

of the farm. Those cocky bastards stood right over there at the edge of the lane assessing its worth."

"Uh oh, what did he have to say about it?" Krystian asks, gesturing toward Nepefan.

"He didn't say anything but I could see him watching from the yard gripping his old shovel like a mad man. God, he had a dark look in his eyes." Nikolai replies, shaking his head.

"Well Papa's seen this before and he knows there's nothing he can do now," says Krystian matter of factly. The men pause, looking out at the farm, as the truth sinks in.

"They visited Jacob's farm too," Nikolai adds, "And every stitch of land in between, I'm sure. Maroushka said she even saw them sniffing around Zelenyy Lis[3]."

"God, they really want everything."

"Tak[4], our whole beautiful world, reduced to a profit margin."

"Here we are under the Soviet's thumb. Why does this feel so familiar?"

"Tak. We know those fingerprints by heart," Nikolai says sadly. He continues, "In 1921, Lenin partially restored private enterprise. But he didn't do it to be nice. He did because he needed to do it if he wanted to remain in power. He did it in the face of Ukrainian Nationalism. We were on the edge of a rebellion."

"He gave us an inch to take a mile!" Krystian says.

3. The Green Forest
4. Yes

"Maybe we should have rebelled," says Nikolai woefully. "There is no such thing as a welcome occupation, remember that."

"I couldn't forget," says Krystian, tapping his leg with his crutch.

Suddenly, Stepan, who has been dozing under a tree, comes to life and speaks. "We've had nearly a decade of prosperity for the common man," he says, running his fingers down his beard, "despite the tainted motivation of Lenin's government," he adds, like an after-thought.

"I didn't know you were listening, or awake," Krystian says with a smile.

"Hush boy," Stepan says, "I'm old but I'm not dead."

The brothers look at each other and laugh.

"Our land was reclaimed, for us!" the old man says, proudly. "It was divided among peasants and farmers. And with that, we reclaimed our ability to take care of ourselves - our dignity. The land, the soil, the sun; that's all a man needs to survive, as long as he's willing to work for it." He leans back in his chair, taking in the farm and the land, as if the view itself punctuates his point. "If a man is willing to work," he goes on, "then he can thrive. And that's a mighty threat to a corrupt government. Why do you think they're propagating a grain shortage? "

"There's no shortage of grain, the grain is here" Nikolai bellows, throwing his arm towards the field. "But we're eating it. We're using it to feed our families. We're sharing and trading with our neighbors."

"There's been no reason for us to sell," Krystian chimes in.

"Exactly! There's no reason to sell," Nikolai echoes. "What would we do that for? For money? We have everything we need right here on the farm, right here in the village."

"We're humble kings," Krystian says, a flash of his old spark, shining through his eyes.

The brothers laugh, surveying the scene and trying to stave off the pain of reality.

In the distance, Nepephan strums his balalaika[5] and Helena kneels at his feet watching his fingers work the strings. Children whoop and holler in play, tearing from here to the back woods and around the barn. Marta and Katerina roll down a grassy slope, then get up and stagger around at the mercy of giddiness and giggles. A group of women are having an animated conversation near the garden. Their collective din reduces to a gentle hum one moment and elevates to a cacophonous roar of laughter in the next.

"We have freedom. And those fucking Bolsheviks can't stand it. They can't just leave us alone to live our lives in peace. They won't allow us to thrive. They want everything that we have."

"They want to take everything!" Krystian says, pounding his crutch into the ground.

Alyona calls out to them, "Come and eat some dessert. I made so much!"

---

5. A stringed instrument with a hollow triangular body

The big wooden table has been cleared now except for a golden loaf of braided bread. A beeswax candle is burning at its center. Katya is serving Alyona's honey cake with fresh clotted cream. Jacob approaches the table now carrying a massive watermelon under his arm. Ivan follows, swaying under the weight of a second watermelon. Both of his arms are stretched around the fruit, muscles straining under its bulk. In spite of the Soviet powers claiming Ukrainian land for collectivization, the celebration continues. The noise of their revelry can be heard throughout the village. It's carried on the breeze up through Zelenilys and on toward the Kobelyiaky river.

12

1930: MAROUSHKA

Maroushka measures two cups of flour and adds it to a big wooden mixing bowl. The piche[1] is alive with low burning coals. She has the kitchen to herself.

I've seen a lot tak. I was raised on this land. And I know the woods better than I know my own skin. I can tell you where to find the sweetest elderberries. I know which herbs and mushrooms are edible. I can heal a stomach ache or induce labor. I know all the secrets of Zelenyy Lis. My mother taught me that. These are treasures that have been passed down to me.

She bends down and retrieves two eggs hidden away in the back of a cupboard behind a stack of plates. She cracks them on the counter and empties their contents into the bowl. She scrapes the inside of the shell with her forefinger and puts them aside to dry. Later she'll grind them up and sprinkle them on the garden.

1. oven

I claimed this land when I was a girl. I could find my way home from the northern banks of the Kobeliaky river in the dark, in a storm or in a thick fog. Tak, I've done all three.

Maroushka laughs and gazes out the window, remembering. She lifts the bowl off the counter and vigorously stirs its contents with a wooden spoon. The ingredients thicken up to form a sticky dough. She flours the surface of the counter and scrapes the dough out -a coarse lump.

But sometimes I think these eyes have seen too much. Sixty eight years. I've seen what war does to men. And it's nothing like what you see painted on a Soviet poster in Kiev. I'm too old for that shit. There is no glory and there is no glamor. It's butchery.

Maroushka kneads the dough, folding and pressing with the heel of her hand. She adds more flour to the counter surface.

It seems like we're at war again. I watched the village men killing their own cattle in the field today. Eleven cows and a bull, slaughtered. Blood sprayed all over the grass and soaking into the soil. I stood at the other end of the field, watching. When the smell of death hit my nostrils I left. This is how they're resisting; slaughtering cattle, destroying machinery, keeping them out of Soviet hands. People are revolting. Claiming power in whatever way they can. It's the sanest reaction to the Russian yoke. That's what I think anyway.

Maroushka moves in a steady rhythm now, spinning, folding and kneading, spinning, folding and kneading releasing her energy into the loaf.

I lost two of my younger brothers in the war. They were boys only. I almost lost my husband Pavlo. He came back to me broken. He didn't speak for a year. I only heard his voice when he woke up screaming and shaking in our bed at night. He took to sleeping in the barn because his terrors were so intense. He was scaring the children. He was scaring me too! But I never told him that.

Maroushka holds her hand to her forehead, pausing for a minute, allowing the memory to move through her. She wipes her eyes leaving a dusty trail of flour across her cheek.

I would join him out there sometimes. Or bring him an extra blanket. And then one afternoon he started telling me his story. All the horrible things he saw. Horrible things he did. How he survived out there. We sat by the fire- the words tumbling out of his mouth in a frantic torrent. Then he would sit there quietly for a long time, head in his hands, shuddering and shaking, tears spilling out between his fingers before the next thrashing wave of words. It was almost like his body needed time to catch up with his story. He was reliving it. He was letting go of all that hell he had been carrying in his being. He kept asking "Why did they have to die like that? Why didn't I do it differently? Why couldn't I be faster? Stronger?" I had never seen a man stripped down to his core like that. I sat there stunned, reverent, listening, feeding and stoking the fire. He finally finished talking as the sun was coming up the next morning. Bahoslovit' Yoho[2]*. Then he went to bed and slept right through the day and the following night. He came back to life after that - mostly.*

Maroushka takes the dough, now smooth and round and puts it into a pan. She covers it with a cloth and leaves it near the edge of the oven to rise in the warmth. This loaf used the last of the yeast. Luckily she knows how to make more, as long as she has access to berries or fruit of some kind.

2. Bless Him

Every day, I choose to live. The Soviets will respond to our resistance by increasing quotas and confiscating food. They're trying to break our spirit. We're already hiding what we have.

Maroushka wipes her hands on her apron and makes her way to the back of the hut. She reaches behind a worn wooden crate that doubles as a chair and pulls out a blue sewing kit. She carries it back to the kitchen and cautiously sets it on the table, looking out the window and then towards the door. It's not often that she has the hut to herself. She opens the latch and lifts up the tray inside, revealing a hidden space in the bottom of the box. She feels around and carefully pulls out a piece of Soviet propaganda. She unfolds the image and lays it out on the table. The picture reveals a healthy, robust and well fed woman working in a field on a collective farm. She has a smile on her face and a shovel full of grain in her hands. Behind her stand other satisfied looking workers and abundant piles of grain. In the background a row of combines move in tandem, harvesting the golden hills in the distance. The message reads, "Let us bring in a rich harvest of new territory."

I ripped this off of a building in the village. Soviet smittya[3]*. I could go to prison for that. They could just kill me, I'm an old woman. They want us to feel like we're heroes for complying - for falling into line. They want us to play our part like good little boys and good little girls. Handing our land over with a gentle smile, submitting to their plans as docile as a new-born calf.*

Maroushka takes one more look at the document, her brow furrowed and her lips drawn into a tight line. She thinks

3. Garbage

about Pavlo and about all the children that will suffer this stain on their lives. Then she grabs a blackened pair of tongs that hang on the side of the oven and carefully lifts the document off the table and places it on the center of the coals in the piche. The paper catches fire quickly and the bright glow dances across her face. She watches the fire burn through the image. It scorches a hole through the woman's face and combines in the distance. The State-owned farm is fully ablaze now. Maroushka turns and takes the cloth off of her bread. She turns back to the oven and nestles the loaf among the coals. The paper has been reduced to nothing but ashes now.

They treat us as cogs only. Measly cogs in their profit-making machine. The more we resist the more they punish us for it. I don't know how to win.

Maroushka takes a seat at the table waiting for her loaf to bake. She finishes the cold dregs of a cup of elderberry tea and wearily rests her head in her hands.

Stalin has ambitions for this country that are beyond sanity. And when you reduce it to its marrow...It's a pissing contest. What will the cost of that be?

13

1931: SEPTEMBER

A wooden cart pulled by two massive oxen makes its way down the main street of Kobeliaky. The combination of hooves and wheels churn up the earth leaving a dusty cloud hovering in its wake. It's driven by a Soviet officer wearing a long gray coat with red lapels. Three more officers follow at a distance, each one carrying an M1891 sniper rifle. The cart comes to a halt in front of a gray building, its decaying frame leaning precariously to the left and threatening collapse. Three distinct groups of men have gathered there. Each group represents a different Collective farm or State-owned farm. Their eyes are hungry, their expressions are grim and their clothes are coated in dust and grime. Ivan and Andrei are among them. In front of them lay burlap sacks of grain stacked into piles The first officer takes a dagger out of a leather holster on his waistband and slices into one of the bags. He reaches in and grabs a handful of grain, inspecting it carefully before allowing it to cascade through his fingers and back into the bag. This man appears to be the leader and the village men watch his expression warily. He nods his approval and an audible sigh ripples through the group. Then they begin the task of loading the bulky sacks into the wooden cart while the officer moves on to inspect the grain provided by the second group.

Dunia is walking towards St. Vladimir's church a little further down along main-street. She is holding her youngest child. Mary is five and she's clutching the edges of an old blanket. The soft gray quilt is the same one that wrapped all eight of Dunia's babies over the last 16 years. It has slowly deteriorated with time and seems to become a little smaller with every wash. When the twins were born it was reduced to its silky edges and Dunia would snuggle it up against their cheeks at night. She wanted to share this piece of love and tradition, made by Maroushka's hands, with all of her children. The twins, born less than a year before Mary, lasted only eighteen days before passing away together in their sleep. Dunia found them cold and stiff in the crib the next morning. She howled with grief and spent three days in bed, going in and out of sleep, breathing in the scent of her babies infused in the old blanket. She would wake up in a frenzy, the instinct to feed her babies blazing, her swollen breasts leaking milk down the front of her nightgown. And then she would remember. She spent hours staring at a spot on the wall where the paint was peeling, interpreting its shape through her grief stricken mind.

There is an old Ukrainian tradition of talking to the dead as if they're still present for forty days after their passing. Having everyday communication and interaction with them in order to say goodbye and tie up loose ends with the spirits of lost loved ones. Dunia would coo and comfort her babies. She would sing to them and talk in hushed tones. Bed time was always the most difficult and she would spend this time like a living prayer. Holding their little souls and keeping them safe, begging for the strength to endure her loss. Early morning, after forty days had passed, Dunia woke up to the warm trill of a willow warbler. She wrapped her shawl around her shoulders and followed the bird's call out into the yard. He sat proudly in the branch of the Ash, unabashedly announcing the arrival of Spring. Later that morning, Dunia watched steam rise off of her garden beds as the sun warmed the earth. She went into the hut and returned carrying the gray quilt. She washed it in a wooden barrel and hung it on the line to dry. That afternoon she breathed in its scent one last time. It smelled like the sun and the wind. She folded it with care, put it away in the cupboard and closed the door. In less than a month, she was pregnant again with Mary.

Mary rubs her chin into the blanket edges now, completely unaware of their sad history. The soft gray blanket used to be whole but is now reduced only to its beloved edges. And this is what Mary calls them...her *edges*.

"What's in those bags Mamo?" Mary breathes.

Dunia leans her ear in as close as she can to decipher Mary's words.

"It's grain, probably wheat." Dunia says, reflecting Mary's quiet tone.

Late last year, the stillness of the early morning was shattered when Soviet soldiers broke into the hut, shouting orders, rifles pointed at the family. This was the Russian's official claim of Dunia and Jacob's land for a collective farm.

Vulnerable and disoriented, Dunia tried to wrap her head around what was happening. The men stood them all in a line and one soldier pushed Jacob down to the ground pressing rifle to ribs. Mary crawled right under Dunia's skirt and wrapped her arms and legs around her ankle like a vice. She trembled there, refusing to let go until the soldiers had finally moved on. Since that time Mary's voice has been reduced to a whisper.

"Where do they take it?" Mary murmurs.

"They store it in a big shed outside of the village for a while."

"Just for a little while?"

"Tak, and then they pack all those bags onto the train and take them to the city."

"Oh." Mary takes a moment to absorb this new information, "why do they take it there?"

"They sell it."

Mary looks at Dunia's face, her expression is one big question mark.

Dunia continues "The people that live in the city buy it and they eat it."

"They eat all of it?" Mary asks, pointing her finger toward the cart.

"No, they sell it to other countries too."

"But don't we need to eat some?"

"Yes we do," says Dunia resolutely.

Dunia and Mary watch as the last sack of grain is loaded onto the cart. The officers shout something to the men and they disperse heading back out toward the fields. There are still several more loads of grain to be surrendered to the Soviet's today. Every time there is a rebellion, every time there is resistance, the Soviets respond with higher quotas, impossible quotas that leave little to none for the villagers of Kobeliaky. Although this group is made up only of men, the fields are being worked by everyone - man, woman and child. There are no exemptions and no exclusions. Mary and Dunia will join them again in the fields shortly. They have only taken an hour to pray. "I hope you understand that it's a privilege," one of the senior officers said to her as she stepped away from the fields with Mary in her arms. Dunia bowed her head, appeasing him.

The first Soviet officer takes his place on the cart and gathers the reins into his hands. He clicks his tongue and the oxen sway under the weight of the yoke. The beasts step forward creating tension between the cart and its attachment chain. When their force is great enough, the cart lurches into motion and continues down the dusty trail past St. Vladimir's and on to the grain store sheds which are heavily guarded by armed officers.

Dunia and Mary move back into the shadows of lilac bushes, watching the cart pass.

"I'm hungry Mamo."

"I know zayushka[1]."

1. Bunny rabbit

Dunia enters St. Vladimirs. They have the church to themselves and in this tranquil space Mary relaxes and uncoils her arms from around Dunia's neck. She climbs down and stands in the entranceway twisting her *edges* through her fingers as her eyes adjust to the light. Everything appears to be in its place. She wanders over to the stoup[2] peering over the lip to see if it still contains holy water. She looks back at her mother and smiles before dipping her finger into the water and making the sign of the cross. Dunia follows. Then Mary makes her way up the aisle and takes a seat on their regular pew. She looks up at the altar and sucks on her fingers. An ethereal yellow light filters in through a stained glass window. The window depicts the image of a holy saint with a warm halo of light around his head. Mary sits, softly hugging her *edges*. She reaches into a pocket on the back of the pew in front of her and pulls out a missal[3]. She runs her fingers along the words and feigns understanding with a soft "hmmmm," and "tak."

Dunia kneels on a hassock and makes the sign of the cross.

Oh Jacob.

A wave of emotion rises to the surface and threatens to burst. She saw him off on the train to Dnepropetrovsk on Saturday morning. After a week of lean rations and the children going to bed hungry, Jacob gathered a bundle of clothes and supplies and left for the city in search of work. Dunia bows her head and presses her fingertips to her forehead.

2. Basin of holy water
3. A prayer book

I'm afraid for him. I'm so afraid and I don't know how to do this alone.

Show him the way, show him the way and show mercy.

Give him strength and keep him under your wing.

Lead him to the right opportunity and protect him from harm.

Bring him home again safe to me.

A tear runs down her cheek and splashes onto the hassock. Her oldest brother Nikolai comes to mind. He's wearing his old brown woolen sweater and a red scarf. She can see him sitting under the massive oak tree on the home farm, writing in his old leather bound notebook.

Will this be my final image of him?

He was deported last year as a political rebel and she wonders if he's alive - if he's doing ok.

"You're always fighting something," Dunia had said to him exasperated.

"And you've got your head in the sand," he replied.

That was how their last conversation had ended. A week later he was gone. Anyone actively resisting the Soviet political agenda was extradited last summer -a total of 1.8 million peasants. This included Nikolai and several of his colleagues at the Ukrainski Holoc[4]. Dunia thought there would be other family dinners, birthdays and celebrations. She thought there would be more time. She thought they had a lifetime together to iron out the rough edges of their relationship.

4. The Ukrainian Voice - A Ukrainian nationalist newspaper

But now he's gone. And all that remains in this moment is a dull ache in her chest and a gnawing hunger in her gut.

Let him be alive, let him be safe.

Dunia pictures her family scattered this way and that like autumn leaves on the wind. She longs to gather them up again. But there's nothing she can do.

Goodness will prevail, goodness will prevail, goodness will prevail.

They stay like that for a time, mother and child, savoring the sense of normalcy the old stone building offers. It could be a regular day. Dunia can almost picture her beloved choir members in their green robes, filtering in from the side room to begin their Tuesday evening rehearsal. She can almost smell the sweetness of a beeswax candle burning on the altar and she can almost hear a murmur of voices - the villagers of Kobeliaky, praying in unison.

14

1932: NOVEMBER

Marta blasts from cupboard to closet gathering warm clothing and supplies and shoving them into a haversack; Dunia's scarf, woolen mitts, a fur hat, a handful of chestnuts she's been squirreling away, a hard heel of bread and an old Horilka[1] bottle filled with water. Katerina is wearing her parka and has a scarf wrapped around her head. Some of her hair has come loose and wisps itself around her face. She ran all the way back from Olena's house with the last piece of information they needed and it stirred her into a frenzy. She's clutching Marta's winter coat and her hands shake with adrenaline.

"Hurry Marta, we've got to go now," Katerina says urgently.

"Help me into my coat," Marta replies.

Marta puts on Jacob's old fur hat and grabs a second bottle off the counter. This one is filled with hot tea. She slides it

1. Liquor

into a side pocket of the haversack which is now resting on Katerina's shoulders.

They burst out into the night. It's after ten and the daylight has long disappeared over the horizon. The moonlight reflects and sparkles off of the snow making the pathway clear. The wind is whipping in from the west, howling through the trees and biting at their cheeks. The snow swirls around them as they lean into the wind.

"Let's take the path through the woods," Marta says, turning around and speaking loudly, so Katerina can hear her, "It'll be safer."

They make their way down through the back field and into the woods. It's quiet in the protection of the trees and away from the scourge of the wind. All they can hear is the crunch of their boots on the hard packed snow and feel the steady flow of their own breathing.

"They're keeping them in that big barn down by Galena's pond," Katerina says.

"Tak," Marta says, increasing her pace.

They travel deeper into the forest where it's harder to see the ground, yet Marta feels more secure than she did out in the open field. She knows this path and has walked it with her mother since she was a girl. She and Katerina grew up exploring these trails and they can find their way instinctively through the blackness. She recognizes the dim shape of a wide stump off to the right. It was what she and her mother called their resting stump. One summer when she was little they sat on the stump quietly watching wild rabbits nibbling grass and clover. She continues along the path across *Ivan's bridge* and over a frozen creek. The water flows down natural steps here in the summer and now it curves and cascades like a flowing ice sculpture. It's called *Ivan's bridge* because Ivan used to run up ahead and hide under that bridge. At the last moment, he would jump out screaming, pretending to be Baba Yaga. Tonight Marta feels immense fear crossing the bridge. She feels like something has carved its way into her chest. She can't move her legs fast enough.

The pathway veers south and runs along the side of a rocky outcrop and down toward another field. Here they swerve east and break trail through the snow, on towards Galena's pond and the old barn.

Katerina leads the way, high stepping through the snow. They skirt the pond and the old barn comes into view. They pause here, peering over the bluff.

"Do you see anyone?" Marta whispers, bringing her mouth to Katerina's ear, trying to be heard over the howling wind.

The barn is dark inside and an armed guard stands outside the door, the red glint of his cigarette flashing like a warning.

"There's a guard," Katerina says, dropping back into the shadows. "Let's sneak around to the back."

"Ok, follow me," Marta says, gesturing to her sister.

They take a wide circle through a tangle of bushes toward the back side of the barn, grateful now for the gale-force wind drowning out the sound of twigs snapping underfoot and brambles ripping at their parkas. They arrive at a sheltered spot. The barn wall is on one side and beside them is a grove of pine trees. Marta can see that the snow has been trampled here. There are at least two other paths leading in through the trees and ending in the same spot where they're standing now. Marta presses her ear up against the barn.

"I can't hear anything," Marta breathes, cupping her hood around her sister's ear.

"Mamo!" Katerina says. pressing her lips against the chink between the logs. In the moment she speaks, there is a break in the blasting wind and her voice rings loudly in the silence created.

"Shhhhhh," Marta hisses, flapping her mitts and putting her hands to her mouth, "Do you want to get us killed?"

"Well what are we supposed to do, Marta?"

"I don't know," she says, holding her hands out in front of her, "Just let me think for a minute." She looks at the side of the barn and notices several sets of tracks that are not their own. "Listen, other people have come back here. It almost looks like someone was digging."

"Who are you looking for?" a voice whispers through a crack in the barn.

Marta drops to her knees and puts her face to the wall.

"My mother, Dunia, she was brought here today."

"Tak," the voice whispers, "Just wait."

Katerina drops to her knees facing Marta, their eyes wide, staring at each other. They kneel there together, waiting. The tops of the pine trees are swaying back and forth. The barn creaks and groans as the wind gusts with force.

"Zayushka?[2]"

"Mamo?"

"Oh my sweet zayushka, I can't believe this is happening, I'm a prisoner here."

"I know Mamo, Olena told us they took you," Marta sobs.

"Oh my girls, I'm so glad you found me."

Marta and Katerina press their faces up against the wood, trying to get closer to their mother. Inside the barn, Dunia is held hostage with fourteen other women.

"Mamo, what are they doing to you?" Katerina asks.

"They're keeping us here, I don't know how long."

Katerina's panic crumbles and she presses her forehead into the barn, weeping into her scarf.

"Is Mary ok?" Dunia asks.

"Yes, she's sleeping now," Marta says, "Maroushka's there."

"Ok, you can't stay here long my girls, it's too dangerous."

"We brought you supplies, warm clothing, food, hot tea," Marta says urgently.

"Here," Dunia says, pushing her hand through a small hole dug underneath the barn wall.

Katerina sees Dunia's fingers and bends down to bring her lips to them, they are cold as ice.

---

2. Rabbit

Marta takes the haversack from Katerina's shoulder and pulls out the bottle of tea. It's the first item they squeeze under the barn wall and into Dunia's hands. She grips the bottle, letting the warmth seep into her fingertips. They stuff each item of clothing through the opening. As she receives them, Dunia bundles up. Hot tears are spilling onto the hard-packed dirt floor, icy with frost, as she gratefully receives the food and water from her daughters.

"I don't want to leave you here," Katerina pleads, still sobbing softly. "Can't we dig you out of there?"

"They know where I live Kat," Dunia says, "They know my family. You have to go. I'll be ok."

"We'll come back tomorrow with more food," Marta says, taking Katerina by the arm and stuffing the empty haversack inside her coat.

Dunia leans her head against the wall and listens to the crunch of their footsteps recede into the night. She sits as still as she can, as if her silence in this moment will somehow keep her daughters safe from harm. She leans back against a wooden pillar. Inside the barn someone is softly weeping. She takes another gulp of the tea and eats the bread.

I thought it was only a rumor. This can't be happening. Olena said that they were asking people to choose between religion and government -that there was some kind of document. They wouldn't do that. That can't be true. But they showed up at my door this afternoon. That was only this afternoon! That happened today! It feels so long ago. They said that I had to choose. I could only choose one and if I chose God I was renouncing the government. It doesn't make any sense! But I signed their document. I renounced the government. I keep seeing myself do it over and over again. Did I do the right thing? Mary was there. Oh God - she watched the whole thing. She watched her own mother arrested! There only seemed to be one choice at that moment. I have taken up my cross.

Her mind spins around, remembering every word, every gesture, the unreality of what happened. She feels herself warming up and eventually, the weight of the day pulls her body down heavily towards the earth. Her thoughts begin to blend and swirl until the sweet relief of sleep tugs her down into oblivion.

Dunia's Prayer

How is this happening?
Here, locked in a barn with all of these
women.
What brought me here?
You were born in a stable. You were
born in a humble place.
And here I am now, in this humble
place… a prisoner.
What's my sin?
I've been loving and obedient. I don't
deserve this.
Where are you Boshe?[49]
If you are so mighty, so powerful, then
do something!
Hear me, help me… help us all. Release
us from this horror.
You've abandoned me. Are you looking
away?
I cannot believe that you would sanction
this mass terror.
Why can't they just dismiss me? Why
can't they overlook me?
I only want to live in peace.
How did my country come to this?
I paid no attention to what was going on
in the halls of power. It was none of
my business.
Should it have been?
And what could I have done differently?
I'm just a simple woman.

Surely I wouldn't disrupt their plans if
they just let me go?

— DUNIA

15

1932: DECEMBER

Dunia sweeps the streets of Dnepropretovsk. She moves briskly down the avenue, her swift actions warm her up against the cold winter morning. A black scarf is tightly wrapped around her head and some of her hair has come free around the edges, coated white with frost. Her breath puffs out before her in a delicate white cloud. Her energy isn't derived from the small dollop of grainy mush glopped into her bowl for breakfast this morning. It comes from something more primal than that –the need to survive. It's well below freezing and if Dunia wants to make it back to the dorm for her sad portion of supper mush, she has to keep moving to stave off the bitter cold.

The dorm is in the wing of an old derelict hospital with drafty halls and thick frost on the windows. The prisoners sleep in rickety bunks or on damp, molding mattresses on the floor at night and go out to shovel snow or sweep the streets during the day. They cannot run. They'll be pursued.

And they're being watched. Each woman is given a black scarf to wear on her head. This identifies her as a prisoner.

The howl of last night's wind finally tapered off and died down in the early morning hours leaving piles of leaves and trash littering the streets. Dunia continues with her unremitting task. Her hands kept busy with the inane assignment. Every morning just brings more leaves, more trash or sometimes a fresh dump of snow. The streets are dry this morning though, and the sky is a startling blue. It's cold and crisp and ice crystals shimmer in the air, made visible in the sunlight. She sweeps around the body of a man huddled, facing the curb of the gutter. His face is concealed under a newspaper and his clothes are caked with dirt. She doesn't know if he's alive or dead. And she can't help him now.

The first time Dunia saw someone dying on the city streets, she tried to help. She pulled him up into a sitting position and wrapped her arms around him in a fit of compassion. He was only a boy, probably thirteen or fourteen but he felt younger, smaller, more fragile, emaciated with hunger. She sat like that with him, calling out to people passing by, thinking of her own sons. But nobody stopped. Everyone on the streets was gaunt with hunger, their eyes intense with their own need. There was no way they could help her and there was no way she could help him. He leaned into her softly and died. She sat like that, cradling his body, stunned. And people continued rushing past, eyes downcast, leaning into the blasting wind. As the boy died, from his own eyes, all was muted and peaceful. He was no longer of this world. When he finally let go, he felt warm for the first time in weeks.

Marta is learning her own set of survival skills. She moistens her lips and sways her hips as she approaches an officer stationed at the barn near Galena's pond. "Hello soldier," she says mildly, leaning back against the wall and gazing out toward the frozen landscape. "I haven't seen you here before, you must be new." The soldier huffs, feigning indifference. "Go home little girl," he says, "Your mother is looking for you." Marta cringes inwardly and remains calm outwardly, a gentle smile playing across her lips. "Do you have a cigarette?" she asks.

Katerina watches from a distance, hidden in the trees. She is so worried her sister will be taken prisoner, or worse. Her heart pounds as she watches Marta smoke her first cigarette. "She's going to be sick," Katerina says to no one. She wonders what's being said, angry and petrified at seeing Marta take this risk.

"We have to do something. We need to find out where they've taken Mamo" Marta had said. "I'm going to go talk to him."

"No," Katerina pleaded. But Marta was determined.

"I'm the oldest," she said, "I have to do this."

At this, Katerina broke into tears, "You can't go," she begged, terrified of losing her sister too.

"Trust me," Marta said, holding her sister's arms firmly and looking into her eyes, "We have to be strong."

Now Katerina watches helplessly from the sideline. The man takes Marta by the wrist. But Katerina hears her sister laughing, making light as she frees herself by spinning out in a twirl, making a dance move out of the maneuver, making it look like play. The two continue to talk. After a long time, Marta finishes her conversation with the man and starts walking in slow measured steps, toward the trees. The soldier watches her leave, a dark and hungry look in his eyes.

Later that day, Marta and Katerina take the train from Kobeliaky to Dnepopetrovsk, carrying bags stuffed with clothes, food and water. The hospital is easy to find once they arrive in the city.

"There she is," Marta says, running up to Dunia, who is standing in line to check in at the hospital. Dunia's, dirt streaked face brightens.

"Mamo," Katerina says, wrapping her arms around her mother's waist and burying her face in her stomach

"My girls," Dunia says, receiving her daughters and looking around cautiously to see where the soldiers are. "We have to be careful," she says in a whisper, "I don't know what the rules are around here."

Marta looks around too, but Katerina remains stuck fast to her mother. She doesn't ever want to let go.

A soldier is standing by, but he's not paying particular attention to them.

"Why are you still here Mom?" Marta asks. "Why are they keeping you? How can they do this?"

Dunia's eyes fill with tears and she weeps into her hands. "I don't know what anything means anymore," she says, trying to get the words out between sobs and shuddering breaths.

"They tell us nothing." Dunia brings her hands to her face and bawls.

"I know, Mamo," Katerina says, trembling. She wants to comfort her mother, she's never seen Dunia so distraught. It's terrifying. At the same time, she's trying to extract comfort from her mother. She could lose her and the reality of that has shaken her to her core. She is still a child.

Finally, Dunia calms down enough to speak again, "I'm just sweeping and sweeping and hoping that one day soon this punishment will be enough, that I can finally go home."

They stay like that, clinging to one another until the soldier approaches, takes Dunia by the shoulders and pries them apart.

"Go home," he says to the girls, not unkindly, "Your mother has work to do now."

Several days later, Jacob sees her too. It happens completely by accident. He's been working in the city since September, sending money home. He's done some odd jobs; digging ditches, doing repairs, lifting and laboring, all for a pittance. One afternoon he steps onto the square and looks up to see Dunia. She's looking right at him. She has been looking out for him since she arrived. It takes a moment for him to realize it's really her. He doesn't know about her arrest yet, doesn't know that she's been brought to Dnepropretovsk. He never expected to see her in this setting and for a moment he stands there stunned, holding her gaze. The moment is surreal and strange; divine orchestration. One minute he's ignorant and the next, she's there before him with her story written all over her; grubby face, hands red and chapped from the wind, eyes glistening with unexpressed grief.

Dunia is equally surprised to see him. She had been looking off toward the southern edge of the square, her attention drawn there for some unknown reason. Then she witnessed a man carelessly throwing his trash onto the ground. A mess she would have to clean up. She experienced all of this, including her own feeling of anger at the man and his thoughtlessness, when suddenly, Jacob is there, in her view. Dunia shakes her head, sure that she must be seeing things. But there he is, looking at her with an equally astonished expression on his face. They move towards each other urgently, side-stepping the other people in the square. Their eyes are fixated, not wanting to lose sight of each other in the crowd. They stand and embrace. Dunia feels herself relax and uncoil as she sinks into the safety of her husband's arms.

"I was arrested," she says.

"What? When? How can that be?"

"They asked me to renounce God and I just couldn't do it. I didn't know that there would be consequences like this."

Jacob is stunned. He looks at Dunia's face, trying to process the situation. He looks down at her hands, they seem smaller than they did before, half the size of his.

"Where are the kids? Where's Mary?" he asks with urgency.

"At home. Marta and Katerina know I'm here. They've been bringing me food and clothing."

"I have to get you out of here," he says, looking around for an escape.

"You can't. They know where I live; they know about the children. What would they do to them if I ran?" Dunia cries. Tears drip down her face, leaving salty white trails in the grime on her cheeks.

"We won't go home; we'll go anywhere else. We'll run; we'll take the children."

"But what kind of life is that Jacob? They need safety. Mary needs safety. Oh God, she's just a little girl."

"Dunia, I beg of you. What do you want me to do?"

"Just wait. I think they'll let me go soon. I mean, what have I done? What is my crime really? They can't keep me here like this much longer."

Dunia can see a soldier watching her from over Jacob's shoulder.

"They're watching me, Jacob. They're watching me right now," she says, looking at the ground.

Jacob looks over his shoulder and makes eye contact with the soldier.

The soldier takes a step forward, a warning.

Jacob looks back at Dunia scanning her face for an answer.

"Go," she says, "They can't keep me here forever."

Jacob hesitates.

"It's okay," she says, "I'm still close by."

Jacob kisses Dunia's hand, "I'll be close," he says. Reluctantly, they separate and say goodbye.

Marta and Katerina come to visit Dunia one morning a short time after her encounter with Jacob. Dunia is frantic. "They're moving us. They're taking us away!" she exclaims.

"What? Where?" Marta cries.

"I don't know. You don't have long; you have to find your father and bring him here. I don't know if I'll ever be back."

"They can't do this, come home with us now!" says Katerina.

"I can't do anything right now," Dunia says, gesturing to the soldiers leaning against the wall, rifles resting casually against their shoulders."

"What do we do?" Marta says.

"Go! Go tell your father. He needs to go to the train station as fast as he can. Go. I heard them say we would be loaded in the next few hours. Hurry!"

Marta and Katerina tear off down the avenue in search of Jacob, who had taken a job brick laying on the other side of the city.

Two hours later, the train whistles its ominous warning. They're leaving. Dunia is huddled inside a train car with several of the women from the dorm. She recognizes some of the women from her first week imprisoned inside the barn near Galena's pond in Kobeliaky. They've been packed in tight and it already smells like piss. A woman is relieving herself over a sad wooden bucket in the far corner of the train car. She sits on the bucket, eyes downcast and her face reflects the shame of her humanity exposed.

"Hurry Dad!" Marta yells as they make their way through the streets that lead toward the station. They dodge a cluster of children begging on the corner and a heavily guarded wagon, laden with grain, near the station steps.

The train whistles again as the engine comes to life and begins its slow chug along the tracks. The train is starting to pick up speed as Jacob and the girls approach the platform. Jacob is in a desperate panic scanning each train car as it passes.

"Dunia!" he yells, "Dunia!!"

But he can't see anything except the shadows of people in the cars passing by. Dunia hears him and calls out but her voice is lost in the noise and chaos; other mothers calling out to their children, other wives calling out to their husbands, an old stooped Baba calling out to God.

As the last car passes the platform Jacob jumps onto the tracks between the rails and chases the train, crying out, screaming; calling for his wife. At last he stumbles and falls down onto the tracks exhausted, as the train barrels off out of sight. Marta and Katerina catch up to him. He is breathing heavily, weeping and writhing on the track. After a time, they lift him up and put his arms over their shoulders guiding him back.

She's gone. She's gone! I should have protected her. Held on and never let go.

How could I let her go? How could I let them take her?

It's my fault. I did it. What kind of husband am I? What kind of man?

Jacob is never the same and he passes away a few months later. Dunia never sees him again.

16

1932: THE JOURNEY NORTH

The train moves west. It passes through small towns and empty fields with their stalks scalped and dry, rustling in the breeze. It passes through villages and past an old dilapidated barn, a face formed in the crumbling structure, with empty windows for eyes and its door shattered inwards to reveal a dark, gaping mouth. The train slices up and around the side of a massive grassy slope and down and around the other side cutting through fresh snow that has fallen on the tracks. As it picks up speed, the snow billows outwards in crystal swirls, the circular motion of the wind made visible by the flurries. Within the train car it's cold and dank. It's hard to tell what time of day it is. The metal frame of the train car is coated with frost and the air is thick with the smell of ammonia and fear.

They travel for several hours, Dunia stands, peeking through the cracks in the cattle car, trying to hold onto a sense of their direction. *I could still find my way back,* she thinks. At last, she surrenders, settles herself onto the floor and leans up against a group of women. The hypnotic chug and clack of the train lulls her mercifully toward sleep. Sometime in the night, she feels the train slow to a steady grind and turn northward, creaking and groaning with its enormous weight. Or is that just a dream? She can't keep her eyes open; she feels weak and dazed, pulled ever downward into sleep. They travel for hours, for days. Dunia loses track, going in and out of consciousness, lost in the comfort of the warm bodies around her. She gets up only once to relieve herself in the bucket. She shivers watching shadows pass rhythmically through small slat windows near the top of the train car. She returns and settles into the disheveled and exhausted heap of women.

It's early morning. A herd of musk deer fill a clearing in the middle of a wood. They've trampled and broken up the snow with their hooves, allowing them access to the moss and lichen, still green and living underneath. A low rumble begins to rise in the distance. The herd takes notice. A few of them raise their heads toward the sound before returning to their meal, digging through the snow with their hooves. The snow and frost has collected on the fur under their chins giving the impression of an unkempt beard. The sound continues to rise and some of the animals begin to shift back and forth restlessly. They are on edge now. Tension moves like a current through the herd. The sound is rolling like thunder now, pressing ever closer to the clearing. An unseen signal tells them instinctively that now it's time to run. They move in unison, taking one last look in the direction of the sound before bolting into the cover and safety of the woods.

The train slows and grinds, rolling its way into the clearing. For a moment all is quiet. The herd has paused and some of them turn around to peer through the trees watchfully, eyeing the train - this roaring mechanical beast suddenly stopped in its tracks. This is the end of the line. From here, only a rugged trail continues northward into the heart of Siberia.

Dunia is awake now. She hears train car doors sliding and screeching open in the distance. She hears dogs barking and growling. She hears men talking in low voices and then shouting orders. She's holding hands with the old woman next to her. The woman's hands are cold and dry -her thinning skin feels like newspaper. Another woman is leaning against her, shaking and twitching, her face buried in her scarf. Dunia searches the darkness for some clue as to what's coming next.

At last their train car door is wrenched open. The sun glares and the women shield their eyes from the blinding light. They climb off the train one by one, staggering and swaying, finding their footing in the snow. They follow each other's tracks and gather in the clearing. They are each given one small wheat cake to eat and a canteen of water. Officers are guarding the space brandishing rifles and hardened expressions.

"Drink it slow," one of the soldiers states, "That's all you get until we're there."

"Until we're where?" asks the woman with the newspaper hands.

The soldier ignores her, "Otherwise you'll be eating snow."

"Where are we going?" She tries again.

The soldier ignores her and moves away further down the line distributing canteens and refusing to answer questions.

On the other side of the train, soldiers are assembling dog sleds, piling them with supplies; food, water, blankets, tools and rope. A shot is fired in the woods. Some of the women scream and cry out. Did somebody try to run? A short time later two soldiers return from the woods dragging the body of a musk deer leaving a bloody trail in the snow. They butcher the animal right there in front of them. Dunia can hear the dogs snarling on the other side of the train, the smell of blood in their nostrils.

When the dogs have eaten their share of the meat, it's time to go. The train hisses, releasing steam. One of the sleds leads the way up the snowy trail in the same direction the train has been going – north. They are meant to follow and walk the rest of the way. A soldier jams his rifle into a woman's back causing her to cry out and stumble forward. The soldier points his rifle down the trail. "Move your ass!" he says. And the prisoners begin to move forward as one. Is it one mile, ten miles, a hundred miles? Dunia doesn't know. All she knows is that they are meant to march. Dunia looks around and sees that there are men among them now. They must have been transported in separate train cars. She scans their faces looking for someone familiar. She sees people she recognizes from Dnepropetovsk and from her time served sweeping but no one that she knows from Kobeliaky. The men look tired and bedraggled with their hair long and hanging oily beneath their caps, and beards grown in thick and matted.

Dunia steps into line and starts to walk. She follows the women in front of her. She follows the path carved into the snow by the big wooden runners of the sled. She follows the footsteps of those that go before her. She breathes. She puts one foot in front of the other. She sees a sparrow hawk circling in the sky. She hears a chipmunk chirping and squeaking in the forest. The sun is low in the sky, but all the same, she feels it warming up the black scarf that's wrapped around her head. The day progresses; they stop for a short time to feed and water the dogs but then the journey continues. People are beginning to weaken, lose energy and fade. By the time the sun has set and a crescent moon has taken its place in the sky, Dunia sees her first comrade fall. It's an old woman that's been struggling to breathe. She falls on the side of the path and rolls down into a tree well. This woman is exhausted. Two people follow her down and try to help her up.

"You need to get up now; it can't be that much further," one man pleads with her, tears in his eyes.

"No!" a soldier shouts, pointing his rifle, "leave her there."

In the hours that follow, Dunia witnesses several more prisoners stumble and fall. She sees other bodies already still and gray, lifeless along the side of the path. To fall is to die.

One of the dog sleds is coming up on her left. She can hear the dog's paws as they land on the snow. She can hear their steady panting. It matches her own. As the sled moves past her, she notices its big wooden runners. They trail out behind the main body of the sled. This sled is piled high with supplies and she sees that she could hitch a ride on the runner. In the darkness, she would be out of the guard's sight. There are two officers at the front of the sled. The first one is holding the reins and steering the dogs. The other officer appears to be dozing. In one swift decision, she steps onto the runner and takes hold of some of the blankets, secured by rope to the sled. She steadies herself and moves with the rhythmic motion of the sled. She's so grateful, she could weep. She stands, feeling the ache and pleasure of rest. She sleeps like that, standing on her feet, clutching the back of the sled.

Several hours later they arrive at their destination.

"Here we are," one of the soldiers shouts.

Dunia doesn't understand. There are no buildings, no tents, just an open clearing and more forest.

"Welcome home," another soldier responds, laughing at his own joke.

Dunia notices stacks of lumber, and several bins filled with tools. There is another pile of supplies covered haphazardly with a brown tarp. The edge of the tarp is whipping back and forth in the wind. The prisoners are exhausted and confused by the situation. Where will they stay? How will they live? Slowly it dawns on them. Understanding moves like a ripple through the crowd. Now, after their grueling journey, they are meant to build the camp that will serve as their prison and their protection from the bitter Siberian winter.

That night, the prisoners stack themselves one on top of the other around a blazing bonfire. They take turns being on the outside, exposed to the elements and on the inside with protection from the biting winds. They take turns piling the cords of wood on the fire to keep it blazing. In the morning, several more are dead, their eyes frozen open, staring at nothing. They are made to stack the bodies off to the side between two snow covered evergreen trees.

"Start a pile over there," one of the officers orders casually.

It's awkward to carry them. The bodies are stiff and frozen. One of the dead man's fingers falls clean off and lands in the snow. Dunia stares at it a moment and decides to leave it where it landed. She sees the woman with the newspaper hands among the dead and silently says a prayer. She wraps the woman's scarf around her head to cover her eyes and trudges back to the fire to warm her hands.

17

1933: KOBELIAKY

LATE FEBRUARY

Ivan's body is pressed up against the cold stone edifice of St. Vladimir's church. His heart is pounding but his breath is slow and even. He knows what he has to do if he wants to eat tonight.

Has my heart grown louder now that my stomach is hollowed out? He thinks to himself.

He is perpetually hungry. No, hunger is an insult to what he is experiencing now - this is starvation. It makes his senses acute, like an animal. He hasn't eaten proper protein in twenty three days. He's counted. The last animal he ate was a rabbit that he caught in one of his traps. But since then, everyone has been hunting rabbits and the colony has thinned out to almost nothing. His traps have remained empty. He suspects that they have been emptied by others as well and he's had to move them around to new hiding spots.

He crouches low, waiting for the right moment. He's thinking about food. It's all he thinks about now. His life has been reduced to the actions he has to take to get his next meal. He can hear the wagon approaching, the clop and thud of horse's hooves on the frozen dirt road. He feels a light snow falling like mist and melting against his face. He closes his eyes for a moment. He can hear the rush of blood in his ears. In a month or two there will be cattail shoots and other spring plants that he can forage for nutrients. He longs for spring as the winter has felt unendingly cold. The world feels much colder without food in your belly.

Andrei and Alex are positioned on the opposite side of the road behind a tangle of barren elderberry bushes. He can't see his brothers now but he knows they're there – poised and ready as he is. Andrei can see the wagon coming into view as he peers through the knot of branches before him. He is silent, watching, like a wolf.

One man is driving the wagon, hands on the reins. He has a full dark beard with a stripe of white running through it. He is watchful, cautiously humming a Russian folk song as he bumps along the road approaching St. Vladimir's Church. The horse's ears have perked up. One of them nickers and snorts, steam coming out of her nostrils.

"Easy," the man says, clicking his tongue at the horses, soothing them.

The wagon is loaded up with makyxa; a firm wheat cake. They are transporting it to guarded sheds on the outskirts of town where it's held for transportation by train to the city and beyond. The country's wheat, grain and other resources are being sold internationally while the country's citizens starve to death. The cargo is covered with a faded brown tarp. Another man sits on the back of the wagon scanning this way and that. He sniffs and pulls his coat up higher around his neck. He's wearing a fur cap and holding a long black whip.

The signal to attack is inborn between brothers. It happens without words or gestures. They are like one animal moving in on their target. In a rush of madness, Alex and Andrei blast out of the bushes. The horses spook and move back in the opposite direction towards the church, moving the wagon out of the frozen muddy ruts in the road. The driver yells out, his focus is on the horses now as he tightens the reins and tries to stay in control. The man at the back of the wagon raises his whip and slashes at the air between him and the boys, producing a sharp *"crack!"* Andrei dodges back and bellows, half yell and half laugh as if to say,

Is that the best you can do?

Both boys are dancing; dodging, darting, feinting and evading the whip.

The horses have tangled themselves up now, trying to escape in different directions. The driver is working with them feverishly, yelling and muttering, trying to regain control and find the way forward.

"Come now, come now," he says firmly, to himself as much as the horses.

The other man jumps off the back of the wagon in pursuit of the brothers, his whip pulled back and ready to snap. In the chaos and confusion, Ivan sneaks up from the other direction and climbs onto the wagon. He reaches under the tarp and finds his prize. He grabs three of them, as much as he can carry. They're big and bulky and he balances them in his arms. He bounds off the wagon back in the direction of the church and to the cover and safety of the trees beyond. For the men on the wagon, the attack seems to end as suddenly and inexplicably as it began. They are left in chaos. The only sound now is the stomping and snorting of the horses and the creak of the wooden wheels shifting back and forth. They turn back to face the wagon and only then realize that some of their cargo has been lifted.

"Kiss me in the ass!" the man with the whip exclaims, throwing his hands in the air and gesturing with blame towards the driver and the brothers who have now disappeared from sight. "Son of a bitch!!" He shouts at the top of his lungs, the sounds bouncing and reverberating off the walls of the church.

"Tak tak. It won't bring them back," the driver replies, wiping the sweat from his brow. He turns away from his angry companion with a measure of patience and moves in slowly toward the horses, grabbing at the reins and clicking his tongue.

The man with the whip kicks at the earth and roughly secures the tarp over the remaining cargo. "Next time, I'm bringing my gun," he says viciously.

Alex and Andrei run between buildings and through a field, taking a wide circle around and back towards their brother Ivan. They meet in an appointed spot in the woods. They've chosen this as their secret muster point during the crisis. If ever they're separated, they can return here to find one another. The spot is marked by a massive oak tree. Their older sister, Marta, had named the tree Lesya when she was little. She would visit this spot often and had taken all the boys at one time or another to meet Lesya, which means, fittingly, defender of man. The tree branches are so immense that some of them have come to rest on the earth. The branches serve as a bench and between the branches are several places to hide.

The boys huddle around in this spot, shoving the cakes into their mouths, frantically filling the void. They know in their minds that it's better to eat bit by bit but their bodies won't allow it. After a time they slow down enough to breathe.

"Those bastards didn't even know what happened," Alex says.

"Son of a bitch!!" Ivan says, imitating the man with the whip.

The boys look at each other and burst into laughter, celebrating their small victory, dissipating the intensity of the evening and feeling the relief of food in their bellies. As the sun goes down, they make their way back to Dunia's hut where some of the family will hunker down for the night, if it's safe. They carry the remains of the Makyxa for Maroushka, Nepephan or Katia if they're there. Kobeliaky descends into the darkness and silence of the winter's night. A tiny sliver of a crescent moon hangs in the eastern sky, emitting a light so small it can hardly be seen.

Throughout a lasting night of darkness
Ne'er shall I rest my own eyes
Always searching for the guiding star
The bright empress of the dark night skies
I shall not allow my heart to fall asleep
Though gloom and misery envelop me
Despite my certain feelings
That death is beating at my breast

— LESYA UKRAINKA ACTIVIST,
FEMINIST, FREEDOM FIGHTER
1871 - 1913

18

1933: THE GULAG

MARCH

It's mid-afternoon and the women prisoner's barracks are empty. The sun shines through the cracks in the crude wood frame lodging, casting strips of light onto a row of beds pressed up together against the eastern wall. Dust motes hang in the air, visible only in each concentrated ray of light. Every bed is a rumpled replica of the next, with a thin gray blanket along its body and a small flat pillow at its head. Across from them, a second row of beds mirror the first. On the northern wall, imposing pictures of Karl Marx and Stalin are framed by a propaganda banner that reads, *Throw the Kulaks Out of Your Way, the Sworn Enemies of Collectivization.*[1]

The room smells like wood-smoke, sweat and the Siberian winter air. The building is topped with a sod roof and

1. Kulak's were successful farmers. Many of them resisted imposed collectivization so Stalin scapegoated them and made them the symbol for everything wrong with the Soviet Union. Entire families were stripped of their land, and sent to exile.

supported by rough wooden posts that stand sentinel near the foot of every bed. Sixty women sleep here. They are a population that turns over daily and monthly as prisoners pass away from exhaustion and starvation. Fourteen hours of hard labor and lack of food define their days and it's not uncommon for two or three women to die in their sleep each night. They are carried out by the other prisoners in the morning and then replaced with new prisoners, sometimes on the same day. There is a steady and continuous parade of new prisoners into the camp and old prisoners into the grave.

The door swings open blasting a rush of cold air into the space. Two officers escort a woman into the barracks. They're laughing and pushing her around. They close the door behind them.

"What's your name?" the first officer asks, leering at her. She is around twenty years old and she's terrified.

"Stefania," she whispers, clutching her coat tightly around her.

The second officer licks his fingers. "Come here," he says.

Stefania watches him warily and takes a step back, her eyes glistening.

"Come here," he says, stepping forward and wiping a smudge of dirt off Stefania's cheek, almost gently. He looks down at her and something dark passes over his face. In one vicious movement, he lunges, prying at her coat and ripping open the front of her shirt, revealing her breasts. He pins her up against a rough wooden post. His hand is around her throat.

"And this will be your bed," he hisses in her ear, twisting her around and pressing her face down into a mattress. Stefania feels the rough woolen blanket against her cheek. She squeezes her eyes shut. She can feel him tearing at her clothes like an animal and hears the sound of her own muffled scream. She can feel the cold air biting at the skin of her thighs. But then something disconnects and she's not present in her own body anymore. She's floating above the room looking down at the scene. She floats higher and passes through the roof of the barracks and up over the gulag. She looks down and sees the snow-covered earth shining in the sunlight.

Outside of the barracks, the other prisoners slog away at their unending labor. A prisoner carries two buckets of water along a make-shift wooden plank walkway, his breath puffing out in a milky cloud against the frigid air. He closes his eyes and sways for a moment, exhausted. The path is dotted with muddy footprints, frozen and filled in by thin sheets of ice. Two prisoners, strapping men, carry a massive log, negotiating its weight and their precarious path along another plank pathway.

"Lift man!" one prisoner says to the other. The vein in his neck pulses as he calls out to his comrade. The life force is still strong in these men. Further south, a structure is under construction. It's a new women's barracks. An old man hammers nails into the side of this building. He is perched on a rickety wooden ladder. His skin is gray. He grimaces and he is missing several teeth. He can barely lift his arm to hold the nail. His light is fading.

"Goner" one soldier says to another from inside the frame of the structure, lighting a cigarette and gesturing toward the man on the ladder.

"I told you already. No man makes it to the four-month mark," the other soldier retorts.

A woman stokes a fire and another one is crouched down, stirring a pot of something. They look like they're old women, even though they are both barely older than thirty. Steam is pouring out of the pot, obstructing its contents from view. A goshawk circles the gulag and from her view, the plank walkway looks like an intricate web set on top of the muddy earth, connecting four separate barracks to a main lodge, to a rickety shit-house and to the well, which is set back in the woods.

A group of men are cutting down a tree in the forest to the west. One man is hacking at the tree with an ax. In his life before the gulag, he was a farmer, he had a dairy and raised seven children. Sweat drips off of his brow. "It's coming down!" he yells suddenly, stepping back. The tree crashes down to the earth sending a plume of snow out in all directions. A soldier sits on horse-back picking his teeth. A rifle is resting casually over his shoulder as he supervises the project.

Further out from the main web, other houses line the periphery. They're prouder than the other buildings. Care has been taken here. One of them has smoke coming out of its chimney. A woman in dark green boots and a wool coat is taking frozen sheets off of a clothes line. She gathers them into her arms and strides up a pathway into a wooden cottage. Once inside, she sets them down and hurries to put another log onto the fire burning in the hearth.

It's dark when Stefania returns to her body. Something woke her up. She can hear women's voices. She can feel the motion of them around her. She's curled up on her side. Her ribs are aching. She sits up slowly and looks around. One of her eyes is swollen shut. She touches it gingerly. Her clothes are torn and her body is exposed. There's blood all over her thighs but she has nothing to clean it up with. One woman approaches and gently presses a cold wet cloth into her hands. Stefania's mind is in a fog and she can't seem to lift herself out of it or fully grasp what she's meant to do next. Seeing this, the woman then directs Stefania's hands, showing her how to clean herself up. She's helped others before.

"I'm Vera," the woman whispers.

Stefania lays back on the bed and allows Vera to fix her clothes and wrap her up in the thin gray blanket. She feels like a child being tucked in for bed. This kindness brings tears to her eyes. She can't remember the last time she felt that way. She closes her eyes. This is where she lives now.

19

1933: DUNIA'S 22ND DAY IN THE GULAG

"LIFE"

Dunia takes the frozen sheets off of the clothes line. They hold their icy shape, sticking out at awkward angles. The sun is shining and the sky is a crisp, clear blue. She breathes in the Siberian air and feels the shock of cold in her lungs. It smells like pine and smoke. She's lucky to be alive. She carries the sheets, stiff as boards and makes her way up the pathway to a neat little cottage. Inside, she sets the basket down on the floor and removes her dark green boots, placing them neatly on the woven straw mat. She hangs the thick wool coat on a wooden hook. Dunia notices the coals burning low in the hearth and hurries to feed them. There is a neat stack of wood, piled up high beside the fireplace. The Official needs the cottage to remain warm. He's not well, although he tries to hide it from his men.

Dunia was brought to him after her third week in the gulag. She was cold and exhausted. She had spent the night out in the open. They were still in the process of building their lodging. The prisoners spent their nights laying one on top of the other in a heap to survive the bitter cold. They kept a bonfire burning, taking turns feeding it. They also took turns suffering the outer positions of the pile, away from the warmth of the fire. Many of her comrades died this way, frozen to death in their sleep. Somehow she slept and somehow she lived.

Dunia prays in the night,

"Dear God, help me to survive this.
Help me to live for another day.
Give me my next breath."

The following morning, Dunia is busy feeding the fire with a spindly pile of kindling she's gathered from the woods, when one of the officers approaches her. "You," he says, "follow me." Dunia is terrified at being singled out, but she follows him. The officer leads her to another man on horse-back. She's never seen this man before. He's wrapped up in a fur pelt. His face is old and lean and his skin is sallow. But his eyes are sharp and he assesses her through gold framed spectacles. This is the Official.

"What is your name mother?" he says, nodding at her.

"I'm Dunia," she replies, heart pounding.

He seems to ponder this for a moment, a smile tugging at the corner of his lips. "Do you know what your name means?" he asks.

"It means life," she says.

This seems to satisfy him and he nods to the officer. Then he gives Dunia a brisk nod, clicks his tongue which sets his horse in motion and heads off in the direction from which he came. Dunia isn't sure what just took place. She searches the remaining officer's face for a clue.

"This way," he says, leading her away from the main area of the gulag. She follows him to another section of the complex, hidden behind a tangled cluster of scrubby trees. Dunia has never seen this place before. She sees that there are, in fact, buildings in the gulag. He leads her to a wooden lodge. It's warm inside and she can smell food. There are several officers gathered around a long table. They're eating and Dunia can't help but stare. She sees a round loaf of bread and a pot of stew. The men are drinking something steaming out of small brown mugs. Dunia drools with hunger. The officers pay her no attention. She gathers a few snippets of their conversation as she's led past them. They're talking about politics, about Stalin and the Russian occupation. She's led further back still, into a kitchen.

"Sit here," the officer says, pointing to the floor. Dunia sits down and leans against the wall, pulling her knees into her chest. "He wants us to feed her first," the officer says loudly. Dunia doesn't understand who he's talking to until she sees someone climbing up from an earthen cellar. At first glance Dunia thinks it's another man.

"Da da, leave her there. I'll call you when she's done," the woman replies. And only in hearing her voice, Dunia realizes that this colossal being is a woman. This is the cook and she runs the kitchen. She's carrying a massive bag under each arm and she sets them down roughly on the counter sending out a white cloud of flour. "Go and sit," she says to the officer, "She's okay here for now." This is her domain and the bulk of her frame dwarfs the officer.

The cook looks down at Dunia and clicks her tongue. Dunia looks down and sees her own grubby hands. There's black grit under her nails. She wonders what she looks like to this woman. She has a sense that the cook must be informed of Dunia's fate. "You stay there now," the cook says. Then she turns away and busies herself at the counter.

Dunia is still taking in the size and muscle of this woman. The cook scoops something from a pot into a small bowl and offers it to Dunia. Dunia wraps her hands around the small bowl and feels her fingers ache as they thaw against its warmth. It's stew with root vegetables whirling in a thick, brown gravy. The cook hands her a small wooden spoon. Dunia eats. It's the best meal she has ever tasted. There are small pieces of meat in it. It tastes like venison and it reminds her of home. She begins to feel warmth in her body for the first time in several weeks.

Next, she's offered a basin of water to clean herself up and given fresh, warm clothes. By the time she's done, the water is black. Dunia feels reborn. She wonders if this is the answer to her prayer or if she's being prepared for slaughter.

The officer returns and leads her out of the lodge and northward up a freshly shoveled path. They pass through a copse of trees, up a small slope, along a natural stone pathway to a small cottage. The officer knocks on the door.

"Enter."

The officer opens the door releasing a blast of warm air. He leads Dunia inside. A fire is blazing in the hearth and next to it on a wooden chair sits the Official. He is examining papers spread out on a small wooden table before him. The officer waits for the Official to look up. Then he salutes him and exits the cabin, leaving Dunia and the Official alone.

The man stands up from his chair and Dunia sees that he is smaller and frailer than he had appeared on his horse. "You will work for me now," he says. Dunia looks at him unsure of what that will entail. "I need you to keep this cabin in order," he continues, "I need someone to clean up and take care of me here. I need you to take care of everything, so I can focus on my work." Dunia nods, assessing the task. She feels energy move through her body, a surge of hope in her chest. "I need this fire blazing and I need you to chop wood. Are you strong enough to do that?"

"Yes," Dunia replies without hesitation.

20

1933: HOLODOMOR

Paftke - a small Ukrainian Village.

Many letters were sent during this time, people reaching out to one another, trying to make contact. Some were seeking a pathway out of the country and a way to survive the war, the starvation and the brutality. Some were trying to connect with their loved ones and find a way toward each other, through all of the madness and turmoil. Others were simply trying to make contact, express their experience and share their truth, perhaps for the last time; an opportunity to leave their story behind. Many of these letters were never received. Some were burned or taken as evidence, while others were simply lost in the chaos; out with the garbage, under the snow or in a pile somewhere, gathering dust - words left hanging and unheard. The following letter was destined for Rzeszow, Poland. The man carrying the letter was passing through a village, 2000 kilometers south of the gulag where Dunia labored. The letter was folded and tucked in his satchel, hidden in a bundle of clothing.

To my dear sister, Halia,

I don't know if you will ever read these words. I will send this letter with a man passing through, to Poland. He leaves tomorrow. I know this is the direction that you headed when you fled. I can only hope and pray that he'll find you there. I told him about the spot you mentioned. Don't worry sister, he's safe. He's one of us.

We are living a nightmare in Paftke. In all of Ukraine, I think. You wouldn't recognize it. You wouldn't recognize me! If Baba were still alive, she would now call me "the skinny one." Even here at the gates of hell, I find myself laughing about that. I think my laughter is part madness -how I carry on so. It's just a way to express... something - maybe something that I can't seem to express in any other way. I want to fight back. I want to scream and tear off the faces of the soldiers that terrorize our village. But I can't do that. Not without a shot to the head. And now, I don't even have the strength anymore.

We do what we have to do to survive. I hope you can understand this...that we do what we have to do to survive.

Baba was always so cruel to you -calling you a princess, telling you that you acted like you were better than the rest of us. Those were lies, Halia. She had her own pain and sorrow and she took that out on you. What an old crow.

Here in Paftke, families are divided; wives against husbands and parents against children. There is nothing to eat. We boiled the hide of a dead horse to make broth. Bohdan and Davyd are still with me. The others...I don't know. We tried to make bread out of some greens that we found in the forest. We mixed them with clay and ground bones. We've tried different things. When you are hungry like this, you'll try anything. It's amazing- this will to live. I've seen people eating grass and dirt. To say we are desperate, well, it doesn't say enough. We are going mad here and the Russians have taken everything.

We had a harvest last year...it was plentiful. I saw it with my own eyes, sister. And they took it all. They are killing us. They only know how to take. They watch us reduced to animals or to absolutely nothing. This is what they are making of us. And I will soon be nothing.

I watched them shoot a man in the street this morning because he looked "too fat and healthy." These were the officer's words. He said, "Where is your secret stash?" And when the man couldn't respond, he shot him. And his blood pooled in the muddy ruts of the road. I would have cried for him if I had any tears left to cry. Instead I sit here now and I laugh....madness.

The streets have become hunting grounds. But not in the way you might think, dear sister. People are hunting children. People are eating their own children. Nobody wants to say that out loud. I'm scared. I haven't seen the little girl from next door in a week. I pray she's hiding inside. Or would it be better if she was gone? Away from this mess. I don't know the answer, Halia. It's taking so much energy to write these words and my brain isn't working properly. I can hardly form a sentence. To make sense of what's in my mind... of all I have seen.

Our dignity is lost.

I haven't resorted to cannibalism yet. I pray you still love me even though I think about it. I think about meat every day, every hour of every day. I thought about it as I saw that poor man dead in the streets today. Those who don't eat will die. Those that share their food will die. I hear stories of others that ate their own children only to die later. How will they reconcile with God in the end? I think about my students. The school is shut down and everyone has scattered. Are they still alive? Who is strong? And who is dead?

I hope you made it out of Ukraine. I pray that you are safe somewhere with food in your belly. Never mind about our fight. I can't even remember what we fought about. None of that matters now anyways.

Someday, if this ever ends, I will meet you back here at the village. I think about that day and it warms me. I will meet you by Ruslana's well on a beautiful afternoon in July. The sunflowers will line the fence with their round faces turned towards the sun. We could run through the forest there like we used to when we were girls. Do you remember? I can see you there with the sun shining on your braid and your fingers purple from picking so many wild blueberries.

I am remembering you like that. You were so beautiful and wild. I'm holding you in my heart.

I need to go now. I am so very tired.

Your sister,
Symona

21

1933: HOLODOMOR; IVAN (14)

The family has come back to the hut to die. They're starving. Ivan is lying in one bed, with his brother Alex next to him. Ivan's eyes are open; they are intense with hunger and need. He's looking at his brother.

He looks so small, Ivan thinks.

Alex's hands are tucked up under his chin, like a child.

We've come home to our beds to die. Ivan thinks. Maroushka, his great grandmother and Katerina, his sister, are behind him, curled around each other in the other bed. Their limbs are intertwined. Nepefan, Ivan's grandfather, is slumped over in the chair.

Is he still alive? Ivan wonders.

His grandfather goes in and out of focus to Ivan's exhausted mind and right now, the man looks like a blur.

Did someone stoke the fire? I feel warmth coming from... somewhere. I thought I heard someone shuffling around. Was that a dream? I can barely open my eyes. It would be so easy to let go. I don't want to die. I'm not ready to die. But I'm so tired.

Ivan begins going in and out of consciousness, like a waking dream.

Mary, my beautiful baby sister. Is that you?

You just faded away after Mamo was taken on the train. I can see you sitting on that chair, in your brown dress with the little deer stitched on the collar. You would tuck your knees in toward your chest and rock back and forth, waiting. You would wait while we went out foraging for food and when we returned, you asked, "Anything?" Always the same question, "Anything?" And when there was nothing, which was mostly the response, you said nothing more.

You waited and rocked - waiting for food, waiting for Mamo to return. Katerina tried to get you up and out of the chair, tried to comfort you, but Mary...you were disappearing. You were always so quiet, but now....well, it was hard to get a word out of you. You were so small and your skin started turning gray. I couldn't save you.

I can feel that motion of you rocking. It's like I am with you now in that moment. I am the little deer, stitched on your dress, rocking back and forth, back and forth, back and forth. I can hear the sound of the wooden chair you sat upon, squeaking with the motion of your rocking– back and forth. I remember waking up one morning and all was quiet – no squeaking chair.

I looked over and saw you, little Mary, my beautiful baby sister with your head thrown back and your hair spread out all around you, eyes looking upwards at...nothing. Silence. I'm so sorry. I wanted to do more; to save you. I would weep for you, if I could. We buried you in the woods. We did our best to do it right, but the earth was frozen and we were so tired.

These thoughts and visions twist their way through Ivan's mind. The hut dims as a big gray cloud moves across the sun. The hut creaks and shifts and settles once again. Ivan opens his eyes and observes his hand, resting in the folds and wrinkles of the blanket. He gets lost in the texture of the fabric. Nothing makes sense. He closes his eyes again and drifts.

Andrei.

I can see you brother. I can see your smile and your dark curly hair in the sunlight. I can see that ratty green sweater that you used to wear, the one with the patches on the sleeves. Mamo patched it up for you so many times and you never wanted to give it up. It was so worn out, but you insisted on wearing it like that. You were always so good - so good-natured and kind. You took after Mamo that way.

I lost you. You took off. When I saw you again near the grain shed, I hardly recognized you. You were so thin. Your clothes were just hanging off of you. And your eyes, I'll never forget the way that they looked that day. You looked haunted. What had you seen?

Later, Alex told me that he heard gunshots. That someone was shot raiding a garden. I never saw you again after that. I'm afraid that it was you -that you were shot. Shot dead scrounging for scraps.

Ivan opens his eyes again. He hears a low moaning. 'What is that?' he thinks, listening, craning, reaching for the sound. It's only then that he realizes the sound is coming from him.

'No, no,' he thinks. 'I can't bear it. I should have been there with you, brother. I should have kept watch. My heart is twisted with sorrow and with guilt. That can't be the way that it ended for you. I won't accept it.'

Ivan rolls over onto his back and stares up at the ceiling of the hut. There is a stain on the roof where it leaked with the last snow melt. He looks at the shape of the stain, trying to interpret some meaning. His heart feels like it's being carved out and his stomach is hollow and still.

'I'll make a new ending for you Andrei. You got away that day. It has to be this way. You heard gunshots and ran as fast as you could. You boarded a train bound for Dnepropetrovsk and then traveled on to Kiev. You met friends along the way. You are living there now, with a gang of boys, causing trouble, raiding and fighting like a man. You got yourself a real gun, a rifle stolen from a soldier while he slept. You are helping the cause and fighting this war.'

Tears leak down Ivan's temples and into his hair, which is shaggy and matted to his head. He's exhausted from thinking. He closes his eyes and drifts.

Papa.

I don't want to call you Papa anymore. I'll call you Jacob. I don't want to be with you. All I feel is darkness and hatred for you. There is something pulsing deep inside my gut - bubbling thick and black like tar. You selfish man! I needed you. We all needed you; Mary, Andrei. You just faded away and left me to try and hold everything together. I can't take care of everybody! I don't have the strength. Half of us are dead. And the rest of us are dying.

I feel like it's my fault. But you should be the one. Here. Trying to be strong! We all lost Mamo to the train. How could you give up and leave me to take care of everything? I don't want to think about you anymore. You're nothing to me. You're dead. I want my Mamo.

The vision moves away from his father and Ivan is now hovering over a wide flowing river. He sees a green, grassy island in the center of the water and birds are nesting on its shores. A family of ducks rest on the island's rocky shoreline, basking in the sun. The mother duck has her head turned around and nestled into her feathers. She is calm and safe, keeping an eye on her ducklings and enjoying the warmth of the sun and the endless flow of the river around her.

Mamo.

I can feel you Mamo. I know you're still alive. I can see you with the light shining around you. Stay strong and live. I'm sorry that I couldn't save you from the soldiers. Save you from your arrest. Save you from the train. I wasn't even there. Where was I? What was I doing at that moment when you were taken away from me? I'm so sorry. I blame myself for it. I'm ashamed. I want to be a man but I'm still a boy. I feel weak and I can't stop shaking.

I remember how it was always so difficult for you to wake me up in the morning. You would try to shake me awake and I would just sleep on and on. 'I slept like the dead,' you said. It's hardly funny at this moment. You're trying to wake me up now. Shaking me. Something is shaking me. Is the earth shaking? Opening up to swallow me whole.

Ivan is pulled up from his vision suddenly. He opens his eyes and sees someone at the foot of the bed. The bed is shaking, lurching forward and back.

"Get up!" Nepefan says, "Stand up!"

Ivan is wide awake now. He can see the old man standing at the end of the bed. He's gripping the wooden posts of the bed and shaking it with all his might.

"Get up!" Nepefan says again, looking into Ivan's eyes. "You will get up out of this bed," he shouts, heaving the bed back and forth, "Go to your Uncle's. He has potatoes. He'll share with you. Save your brothers and your sisters. You'll find food. You'll find a way to live. Get up!"

Ivan sits up in bed and the spell is broken. His grandfather comes into focus.

He can see the old man's grizzled face and the wiry muscles of his arms. He sees an intensity and a fierceness, in the man's eyes, something he's never seen before.

Nepefan continues lurching the bed back and forth.

Who are you? Ivan thinks.

It's like a dream, or like waking up from a dream. Ivan feels like he's seeing this man for the first time. He's never known Nepafan as a warrior. By the time he was born, the man had sweetened and softened with age. He heard stories from his Uncles, from his mother, from Maroushka and he sees it now. This man is not going to let his family die like this. He simply won't allow it.

All at once, Ivan agrees. He's not going to die here in this bed. He has a strange glimmer of his life on the other side of this horror. He sees himself as an old man with children and grandchildren around him. It's not going to end like this. In an instant, he knows it.

Alex is awake now too, staring at his grandfather.

Nepefan stares back at his grandchildren with a half-crazed look in his eyes, hair standing up in all directions, in great white tufts.

"Get up," he says again. "Stand up and live."

22

1933: DUNIA

MAY

"You'll never grow anything here," the soldier says to Dunia. His name is Osip. Dunia has started to recognize some of the officers and soldiers in the Gulag and know them by name. "Siberia is not a garden, the soil is very poor... hard...crusty...dead!" Osip punctuates each word with a wave of his hand. Then he leans back against the fence lazily, watching Dunia work. Dunia is busy digging into the earth. She is clearing a plot of land, turning over the black soil. It's a warm day and Dunia has taken off her wool coat and hung it over a wooden fence post. She can smell the rich, dark fragrance of the earth mixed in with the spice of her own sweat. It reminds her of home.

"Kobeliaky," she says lovingly under her breath. She thinks about her children for a moment. She remembers Marta's face when she was a little girl; how rosy her cheeks would get when she was tired. But then she stops herself. 'I can't think about that right now.' She risks falling apart if she does. Dunia picks up a stubborn clump of dirt and breaks it apart with her hands, freeing a small brown earthworm. The texture of the soil brings her back into the moment. The officer continues to watch her work, relishing the spring sun streaming onto his face. "Well, if you want to waste your time, then go ahead and do it," he says, poking around for a response. Dunia only pauses to look at him a moment before returning to her shovel. "Don't you have enough work to do? I'm amazed that Alexander is entertaining this foolishness," Osip continues, shaking his head. Alexander is the name of the official. Dunia learned this shortly after she moved into the cottage, three months ago. The soldier calls him by his first name only here at a safe distance from the man himself. Within earshot Osip refers to the official, only as "Sir."

After a while Osip grows tired of Dunia's placidness and wanders back down the path toward the main body of the gulag. She is relieved to see him go. There are many different personalities among the officers and soldiers and now that she's not suffering malnourishment and being worked to death, she has the ability to recognize these subtleties. Osip is harmless to her, under the protection of the official, but he's slothful and small-minded. He often wanders by, looking to waste time and watch her work. He's an arrogant man. Dunia appeases him and sends him on his way by listening quietly, remaining calm and saying very little. 'Tishe yedesh; dalshe bude,'[1] she thinks to herself, as the man disappears from sight.

1. If you ride quietly, you'll go farther (an old adage in reference to hitching a ride in a cart.)

Dunia wants to finish turning the plot while Alexander takes his nap. Three days ago, he presented her with a basket full of seeds. She was surprised by his offering.

"You want a garden then?" she asked.

"Your duties around here come first," he said, gazing at her with cool gray eyes and hooking the basket over her outstretched palm, "this is not a summer camp!" The man turned and walked away without another word.

Dunia looked down at the basket, examining its contents with curiosity. She had brought up the idea weeks ago.

"I could grow some vegetables if you want," she had said one day, as she was sweeping up the stone pathway and looking out on the yard. Alexander sat on a wooden stump polishing his rifle.

"I doubt that," he said, without looking up.

"Fresh vegetables would improve your meals too," she went on, naming the dishes she could prepare with fresh produce, "Holubtsi[2], vereniki[3], pickled beets." When he didn't respond, she left it at that. She thought the whole conversation was forgotten until the day he presented her with seeds.

Dunia feels the breeze blowing across her face. She hears it swaying through the pine trees. She wonders why he did it. Maybe the thought of her culinary dishes enticed him. Maybe he was curious to see if vegetables could actually grow out of the cold, hard, Siberian earth. He may have also considered that fresh vegetables might help heal his condi-

---

2. Cabbage rolls
3. perogies

tion. Alexander always has a reason for his action. He calculates. He considers possibilities and analyzes risks. He's made his career out of it. But illness was not part of the plan. And Dunia can see how he resents it.

"I didn't agree to this!" he cried out one night, when he was in particularly bad shape.

The sun is starting to lean west and Dunia has carved out a small piece of land. The soil is beautiful, Dunia thinks, though different from her garden in Kobeliaky. Tomorrow she'll inquire about manure from the horses. As she moves from side to side, turning the earth, the front of her apron rattles. There are six envelopes with seeds in them – cabbage, carrots, potatoes, onions, beets and beans. Everything she needs to make Borscht. They were brought in with the last influx of prisoners and supplies. Dunia imagines that they came from an old Baba's garden and traveled to her in the hands of a soldier that knew nothing of their destination or their potential. She sees them tucked away warm in his pocket as he rides along on the dog sleigh through the dark, cloudy, starless Siberian night.

Dunia knows she is extremely lucky to be where she is - to be alive. And she knows that less than a kilometer down the path, her comrades are suffering. She hears shrieking sometimes. She smells decay and rotting flesh. She struggles to reconcile it. 'Why should I be *here,* while they are over *there*?" she asks herself, and God. Sometimes she's wracked with guilt and agony and at other times, she lets it all go; too tired to hang onto anything that doesn't belong to her. She pares life down to the task in front of her. She does it completely. It helps her to stop thinking about what's happening a short way down the path. Dunia takes out the envelopes and examines their contents for the fifth time. She's always in awe at the living potential vibrating within the shell of a tiny seed.

Looking skyward, Dunia wipes the back of her hand across her forehead and reluctantly submits to her instincts. They are telling her to check on the official and leave her garden bed to rest for the day. She enters the cottage and stokes the fire. Alexander rolls over in bed and looks at her. He sits up slowly and rubs his eyes. "Water," he says. Dunia brings him a glass of water and sits on the wooden chair beside the bed.

"How do you feel?" she asks.

"Fine fine," he says, wincing. Dunia doesn't know what's wrong with him but his skin is gray. He's always cold and he seems to be getting smaller every day. She wonders how long it will take for him to admit his condition to his men. Or, for the men to admit the condition they see written plain as day across the man's face. Dunia is grateful for their denial. Her life depends on keeping Alexander alive and well.

23

1933: GARDEN IN SIBERIA

AUGUST

Dunia stands barefoot in the soil. The sun is rising and casting its light in flames of color through the thin lines of dappled cloud cover above her. She's been coming out to her garden in the early morning for a week since the rain stopped. It's the only time she is guaranteed solitude. She comes to feel and to pray. This is her church now. Her face is tear-stained. But her sadness has finally led her into stillness. She looks up at the sky streaked with orange, magenta and deep purple. All is quiet. Dunia watches the colors shift and change like a living work of art. She's surrounded by the silhouettes of the massive plants in her garden. To her left the carrot greens are now almost to her knees. Behind her a row of enormous cabbages line the west side of the garden. Before her are several more rows of potatoes in raised beds with thick luscious greens picking up the reflection of the sky in their striated leaves. And surrounding it all, the spruce trees stand like sentinels. Dunia's never seen vegetables grow like this. It's an act of God, Dunia thinks. A garden always is, but this is inexplicable –a sumptuous garden in Siberia.

It rained heavily for the first half of August and Dunia watched as her garden plumped up. Then, after all the rain, the sun showed its face through the clouds one afternoon and shone down steadily for the next week. Dunia watched in awe as the plants grew from one day to the next. Leaves grew broader, roots grew thicker and shoots rose higher. She wasn't the only one watching. Rabbits and deer, soldiers and officers all took notice of the fresh vegetables and wandered by looking for a snack. At this point, a wire fence has been erected to keep out the animals. As for the men, Dunia sent them away with the wave of a shovel or a broom saying, "They're not ready yet!" or "These are not for you!" On one occasion, Alexander assisted her with the threat of his rifle.

A robin breaks the silence with its morning song. Dunia looks toward the sound and sees his stunning blue color as he perches on the top of a giant Siberian Pine. He welcomes the day with his warbling interlude. She can feel it in her heart. Dunia drops to her knees and begins loosening the soil around a carrot. She digs around its top, takes a firm grip and pulls upwards - release. She brushes the dirt off with her hand and eats. It's sweet and crisp. It tastes like the earth and the sun and life. Jacob always said that this is how carrots are meant to be eaten. Thinking about him gives her strength. She pictures his face, his strong hands, his beautiful skin tanned by the summer sun. She tastes the dark grit of the soil on her tongue. When she's done, she moves to the next carrot in the row and then the next. Then she digs up several potatoes and beets. She gathers her ingredients in a straw basket as she moves from one section of the garden to the next. Lastly, she picks out the big green cabbage. Today, she'll make Borscht.

Dunia carries her basket to the cabin, quietly sets it inside the door and comes out of the cottage carrying a pair of muddy brown boots. She puts them on, grabs a wooden bucket and heads north up a narrow path through the woods. The sunlight comes in sideways through the trees now sparkling off of dew drops resting on the beech tree. She sees scraggles of Old Man's Beard growing off the branches of pine trees and smells the living earthiness of the forest floor. It's thick with moss. Dunia can still see the little yellow mushrooms that had popped up overnight, seemingly out of nowhere, when the rain was heavy. Some of them are still thriving in the well-shaded spots.

Dunia sees an enormous, dark brown fungus growing on the side of a fallen tree. She recognizes it as Chaga. Her Baba, Maroushka, taught her about this medicine and how to prepare it for healing. She can picture Baba now, brewing a pot of Chaga tea in the outdoor kitchen at her parent's house in Kobeliaky. She's wearing her dark green apron and adding other herbs to the brew. Her cheeks look round and soft. Dunia can hear her sing-songy voice and see the wrinkles around her eyes, as she smiles. Dunia feels the connection and remembers what to do. She harvests several pieces and puts them in her apron to take back to the cabin to prepare for Alexander.

As she walks further into the woods, she hears the sound of water burbling up ahead. The stream has calmed down since her last visit and the water is running clear again. She squats down and watches the water bubble and splash, pouring endlessly over the rocks, to God knows where. After a time, she bends down and washes her hands and face in a swirling pool. She lays face first on a flat rock, careful not to crush the treasures in her apron, and drinks directly from the stream. Then she collects fresh water in her bucket and heads back toward the cabin enjoying the music of the water receding behind her as she follows the path homeward.

When she returns to the cabin she begins washing and chopping vegetables. She admires the size of the cabbage. "This cabbage is as big as Osip's head," she thinks before bringing her knife down and chopping it into fine shreds. She's built a fire outside to cook her Borscht. "It'll taste better this way," she says to Alexander when he asks her about it. It's warm enough now that she prefers to do all her cooking outdoors. It makes her think of home.

She's not responsible for all of Alexander's meals, as the cook will provide food whenever he asks for it. But now that her garden is ready for harvest, she'll cook more and fulfill her promise to him of healthy meals with fresh ingredients. She has even foraged the forest for other fresh herbs and morsels to add to her cooking. Now, she melts suet, borrowed from the cook, in a large pot over the coals of the fire. She has access to such ingredients only because of the official's rank and position. She adds onion and stirs it around as it fries and sizzles. Slowly she adds other vegetables. Her morning goes on like this in her outdoor kitchen and she gets lost in her creation. She hums a tune that she had forgotten for a long time. It's a song that she used to sing with Olena back at St. Vladimir's church. It came to her like a gift as she built the fire, and it's been with her ever since. She wonders where her childhood friend is now. Did she send her this song from the other side? Dunia knows that many of her loved ones must have passed on now, but she still feels them nearby.

Alexander is up and leaves the house to meet with his men down in the main body of the gulag. By the time he returns, gray and exhausted, the soup is bubbling gently over the fire and a smaller pot of dark Chaga is brewing beside it.

24

1933: THE DREAM

That night Dunia has a dream. She dreams that she is standing on the edge of the back field in Kobeliaky. It's their field but it's different somehow; untended, green, lush and overgrown with gnarly trees. Jacob is standing in the middle of the field. He's wearing his church clothes and his hair is combed back. Dunia can see in the distance that the forest is on fire. The flames are enormous, reaching skyward into a swirling black void. Jacob can't seem to see her. She tries to call out to him but struggles to form words or make a sound. Dunia looks down at her hands and sees that they're bound together with rope. The rope is alive and when she tries to free her hands it only grips them tighter. It continues wrapping itself around her hands, layer after layer of rope until it looks like she's wearing a pair of bee hives on her hands. When she looks up again, she sees a colossal boar emerge from the trees and move slowly toward her husband. Jacob is dwarfed by the immense beast and when its tusk makes contact with him, an orange cloud swirls up toward the void in the sky. She watches spellbound as the color churns and eddies until it's lost - absorbed into darkness. When she looks back again to the spot where he stood, a wooden cross stands in his place.

The intensity of the scene shakes Dunia from her sleep. She hears the echo of her own voice in the cabin and wonders if she has shouted out loud. She lays quietly, listening. She hears the steady sound of Alexander's breathing from the other side of the cabin. She shrinks in toward herself and pulls the blanket up to her chin, chilled by the terrifying image. She stays awake like that for hours as the dream gnaws on her. She can't stop turning it over in her mind trying to make peace with what she saw. She tries to negotiate with her vision. Change it somehow. Give it a happy ending. By the time the soft light of early morning has pierced the darkness, Dunia has faced an unwelcome truth. She knows in her heart that her husband, Jacob, is gone.

25

1934: PLANTING SEEDS

JULY

The story of Dunia's garden spreads. An officer shares about it on the train as he travels back to Moscow for his new assignment, "This prisoner planted a garden and well…I didn't think anything could grow up there," he says looking out the window at a field of golden wheat. His comrade looks up at him doubtfully and goes back to shining the side of his rifle with an oily cloth.

A soldier boasts about it while drinking Samogon[1] with his family, near Saint Petersburg. "It's a fucking wasteland, it's a fucking wasteland," he shouts, slamming his glass down on the wooden table. "And we were eating fresh grown Siberian vegetables!"

One morning, several weeks later, a high ranking general visits the gulag. Dunia overhears Alexander and another officer talking about the general taking a special trip from Moscow to "assess the conditions" of the camp.

1. Home-made moonshine

'They make it sound like a humanitarian mission,' Dunia thinks, shaking her head and swallowing another lump of anger. She walks up the path away from their conversation. She can't listen to them talk anymore.

To survive her circumstances, Dunia focuses on her simple life in the cabin. Sometimes she loses herself in weeding the garden or cooking a meal or tending the fire. And sometimes, mercifully, she forgets where she is. Then the sudden blast of a rifle or the scream of a comrade knocks her back to reality. Sometimes the wind blows north from the gulag and carries with it the smell of rotting flesh. It reminds Dunia of a pungent truth – she is still a prisoner here.

Dunia is grateful the official chose her to be his housekeeper. He saved her life. She's grateful she was spared death by starvation or by labor or by something much worse. But many of her comrades haven't been spared. And where are her children? Have they survived? Her family is suffering somewhere far away and out of reach. It's too much to think about and even more dangerous to have feelings about it. Her people are suffering. And Jacob is dead. Somewhere along the way a seed of hatred has planted itself deep inside Dunia's belly. She prays for God to help her to dissolve it. But it continues living and growing inside of her, like thorn covered vines, tangled together, writhing in on themselves and intertwining into a poisonous mass.

Dunia grabs the ax from the side of the cabin, raises it above her head and brings it down, *crack,* onto a pine log. It splits in one chop. "I love when that happens," Dunia says, cheeks flushed pink. She raises the ax again and splits each piece into smaller kindling. She has gotten skilled with an ax. Her work has made her lean and strong. She notices the muscles in her arms as she brings the ax down again and again, *crack, crack*. "This is helping," she thinks, raising the axe skyward, "Damn you Stalin," she yells, *crack!*

After his day in the gulag and a meal in the officer's lodge, the General walks purposefully up the path behind Alexander. "I want to see this garden I keep hearing about," he says. Dunia is stacking wood near the front door of the cabin when she hears them coming into the yard. "Dobryy den[2]" the general says to Dunia.

"Dobryy den," Dunia replies, noticing how strange the greeting feels in these circumstances. master and slave greeting each other like neighbors. The general nods and turns to examine the garden. He squats down and picks up some soil, rubbing it between his fingers as it falls to the earth. Then, he examines an enormous cabbage. His eyes scan the green beans and follow the plant's hearty tendrils upward, round and round a standing trellis, over six feet tall. He clicks his tongue.

Dunia wipes the sweat off of her brow and continues to watch him, unsure of her part in this exchange. 'Why is he interested in the garden?' Dunia thinks, 'what does he want here?' Dunia is so tired of anticipating the needs of these men. She puts her hands on her hips and then feeling the power in her stance, lets them slide back down to her sides once again.

The general stays late into the evening. The northern lights move across the sky like a green snake, slithering forward

---

2. Good afternoon

and back and then disappearing, only to reappear again in the distance. Dunia lights a fire outside and the two men sit and talk quietly over steaming mugs of chaga.

In the morning, Dunia learns that Alexander is leaving the gulag. He's retiring and moving back to Moscow where he can rest, while his daughter takes care of him. Dunia didn't even know that he had a daughter. 'I wonder if that's why he was kind to me?' Dunia thinks, 'Do I remind him of her?' She learns that she's leaving too. Arrangements have been made for her to transfer to an experimental farm near Moscow. She's sure that this decision has been made with Alexander's influence. It's his way of saying thank you.

26

1934: THE EXPERIMENTAL FARM

AUGUST

Dunia bumps along in the back of an old, blue truck. She's traveling down a roadway somewhere south of Moscow. There are two other passengers bouncing from side to side with her. The passengers take turns observing one another over the course of their journey from the train station in Moscow, south through the Russian country-side. As the truck lurches along, the wind whips Dunia's hair this way and that. She is mesmerized by the scenery. 'I can't believe life has continued on while I've been locked away in a gulag for the past two years,' she thinks wistfully... resentfully.

The sun is blinding and Dunia shields her eyes as they pass by an orchard where pears and apples are hanging off the branches of the fruit trees. There's a small stand set up on the side of the road where a farmer and his wife have set up boxes of fruit and vegetables for sale. Dunia can make out shiny red cherries, purple cabbage and yellow melon, as the truck whisks past. Another hour down the road, they pass a pond so thick with white swans, that from a distance, Dunia thinks she's seeing snow in the middle of August. They drive over a bridge and Dunia leans out to see a wide green river with a muddy shore. Two children are paddling a dinghy across. A boy squints up when he hears the truck rattling across the bridge and shouts something. The road moves up and down the rolling hills. The grass ripples in waves. Soon the truck slows and turns onto a narrow roadway and drives directly through a field ripe with watermelons. A group of people is gathered in the shade of an oak tree and they stand up on seeing the truck, as if awaiting its arrival. This is where the truck finally comes to rest. Dunia peeks over the side and watches as a foreman steps forward from the group and greets the driver.

"Do you need water?" he asks.

"Yes. And for the passengers too," the driver responds, climbing out of the truck and stretching his arms up over his head.

The foreman shouts and signals to a young man that approaches with a colossal jug of water. The driver drinks deeply and wipes his mouth with the back of his hand. Then he opens the tailgate and passes the jug to Dunia. She drinks and passes it to the other passengers. Dunia climbs out from the back of the truck carrying a small bundle of clothing -her only possessions.

The foreman calls out to the group of people that are scattered around him, "Ok, let's get this load in and then we can break for the day." Three workers climb up into the back of the truck and the others start picking ripe watermelons from the field and passing them up into the truck. Dunia stands back, waiting for instructions.

"You too," the foreman says to her, "You can help us here and then we'll take you up to the house."

"You two can stay in the truck for now," he says to the two other passengers. "This one will show you what to do," he says, gesturing to another worker climbing up into the back of the truck.

Dunia sets her bundle down next to a lone tree and moves toward a big green melon resting in the field. "Tatiana!" The foreman shouts, getting the attention of a young woman with a red scarf around her hair, "Show her what to do." The woman makes her way over to Dunia and nods at her. Tatiana squats down next to the melon, tucking her skirt between her legs and turning the melon's underbelly upwards so Dunia can see it.

"So what you're looking for is a creamy yellow spot where the melon rests on the ground. So this one is ready, can you see that?" she says, circling her finger around the spot and checking to see if Dunia understands. "Now come over here and look at this one," she says, moving towards a different watermelon. "This one's not quite ready…do you see the difference?"

"Yes, I got it," Dunia says.

"And one more thing," Tatiania says. "Do you see this curly tendril that connects the melon to the main vine? This one's still green," she says, pointing to the second melon. "That tells you it's not quite ready. But if we go back to the first melon, you can see that the tendril is brown and dry?"

"Yes."

"Well that also tells you that this juicy melon is ready to eat!" Midway through this sentence, Tatiana's demeanor completely changes and to punctuate the words "juicy melon!" she grabs a hold of her own breasts and squeezes them upwards turning for the crowd to see. Several of the women laugh and Dunia is completely taken aback by the woman's behavior. She stands there unable to respond. She can feel the heat of shame and embarrassment creeping from her chest all the way up her neck to stain her cheeks pink.

"Ok, that'll do," the foreman says to Tatiana. The other women continue tittering, their jest fueled by Dunia's discomfort.

Tataiana takes one more amused look at Dunia and heads back down the row to where she was stationed before. Dunia stands there stunned, watching the woman retreat. 'What place have you brought me to, God?' Dunia thinks, bending down and freeing a watermelon from its vine. She scoops it up and hands it off to a woman that is passing melons up to another woman in the back of the truck. It's only then that Dunia realizes that, aside from the driver, the foreman and the waterboy, women make up all of the other workers. She missed it at first, as several of the women are wearing trousers and have their hair pulled up under hats or scarves. Dunia starts to learn some of their names. There's Vishnya, which means cherry and Tatiana, who she already had the pleasure of meeting, and Medovyy, which means honey.

'Are these real names?' Dunia asks herself wondering if she is again the butt of some elaborate joke. But as the day wears on and the truck starts to brim with melons, Dunia learns that the lewd language and sexual jokes are not reserved for her. This is how these women talk to each other, referencing their breasts and pussy- not only to each other, but to the foreman too.

"I'm wet all over," Vishnya says, looking at the foreman and wiping her scarf between her breasts suggestively.

"Okay ladies, we're done here now," the foreman says, seemingly unaffected by the comment. The truck driver is hanging out of the driver window fully enjoying the display. The foreman hits the back of the truck, calling the driver to task and indicating that the truck is fully loaded and he can now head back the way he came. It's clear the man would like an invitation to dinner but there is none. Reluctantly, he puts the truck into gear and drives off slowly along the narrow path leading to the road and out of sight. Dunia stands there resisting the urge to run after him. She wants to escape and hitch a ride back to anywhere. Anywhere more civilized than this place. She has never met women like this. She has never heard women talk this way and it's completely knocked her off center. 'Such Godlessness,' Dunia frowns, 'And from women's mouths.'

Once the truck has disappeared down the road, Dunia gathers her bundle of clothes and starts following the scattered trail of women making their way to the edge of the field. They follow a path through the woods, to a large red brick house. Dunia is led inside and shown to her quarters. She's sharing a room with three other women. It seems the men have separate quarters as they continue walking past the house towards another building in the distance.

The smell of food wafts in through the hallway and Dunia's desire to eat conquers her desire to run. She hasn't eaten a bite all day, except for a handful of wild blueberries she found when the driver stopped so they could stretch their legs for a few minutes along the road. She follows the other women down to a mess hall with a long wooden table. She takes a seat and food is passed around in a frenzy of shouts. "Pass that here," one woman shouts. "Hey, that's enough for you Halia!" one woman says gesturing to the amount of stew in another woman's bowl. Dunia gets her elbows in there to get what she needs. She's hungry and she's not going to miss this meal. It reminds her of her brothers coming in from the fields famished from a day's work. Dunia digs into a bowl of stew filled with garden vegetables; carrots, potatoes, herbs and slices of hard-boiled egg. She bites into a piece of bread torn off of one of the loaves being passed from hand to hand around the table. For dessert, an immense watermelon is sliced into rounds, quartered and plopped down in the center of the table. Dunia bites into it and the juices run down her chin. She's never tasted anything so sweet.

27

1935: OCTOBER

SONG

"Ku-ku-ri-ku!" The sound enters Dunia's dream and pulls her up, up toward consciousness. She was somewhere and now it's lost, the image fading softly into darkness. There was water. Was it the sea? She remembers the sound of crashing waves.

"Ku-ku-ri-ku!" up, up she's pulled from the misty depths, up toward the day. Dunia rubs her eyes and sits up on her elbow, squinting at the sun pouring in through the window. 'I was just there a moment ago and now it's gone.' Dunia thinks. She lays back and luxuriates in the warmth of her bed. For some reason she sleeps so deeply here. She's not on call at night in the same way she was with the official. She was always hyper aware of Alexander's needs and the unbreakable bond between them and her own survival. And now here, in this place, she's let that go. The rooster wakes her up every morning. She looks over at Tatiana, who is still snoring softly, mouth agape and arms thrown up over her head. The rooster wakes up Dunia and Dunia wakes up Tatiana. That's how it seems to go.

"Give it here!" Tatiana says in response to her own dream, as Dunia shakes her awake. Tatiana opens her eyes and looks at Dunia, confused by the void between sleep and wakefulness. Then she rolls onto her side, tucks the blanket under her chin and watches with a vacant morning stare, as Dunia dresses for the day. Dunia feels more comfortable with her own body, after three months spent with these women, than she has in her whole life. They have no shame. They strip down naked in front of each other without batting an eye, and refer to their own bodies with a vulgarity that could make a hardened soldier blush. While it's been shocking, it's also dissolved something for Dunia. She's been educated. She knows more about her own anatomy than she ever learned in her early schooling in Kobeliaky. Religion taught her to cover up and to feel shame about her body. But it's more than that. Dunia knows Tatiana's story now. Knows what she went through and what led her into the life that she's living. It wasn't pretty. Dunia disapproves, but she also accepts. She wonders to herself, 'was it actually God's intention for me to live in shame about my own body? For some reason, God has dropped Dunia down into this place with these women. Prostitutes, many of them, and other lost souls brought here to recover or to escape. This was done on the back of someone's good will. Dunia hasn't figured that part out yet. The farm is mostly a safe place for these women. Dunia has never felt threatened here. Not by a man at least.

Dunia kneels before her bed and prays quietly, "Heavenly Father, thank you for this day and for my restful sleep. Thank you for sparing me from the gulag. Show mercy to all my comrades that are still suffering. Shine your light on the faces of my children. Show me my purpose in this place. How can I help these women? Guide my words and actions today."

"Is God listening?" Tatiana interrupts, "Or is he distracted!" she says referring to her own body as she sits up in bed and stretches her arms over her head, letting the covers fall down all around her.

"And help me to be patient," Dunia continues, increasing her volume and looking pointedly at her friend.

Dunia stands slowly, making the sign of the cross, a smile tugging at the corner of her lips. "I believe that God is everywhere all at once," she says, opening her arms to encompass everything in the room, including Tatiana's nakedness.

"Thank you mother," Tatiana says with equal parts love and mischief. The title started out as a joke, Tatiana's sarcastic reaction to Dunia's disapproval of her bawdy behavior, but as time went on and affection grew between them, Tatiana started calling Dunia "mother," in earnest and some of the other girls have adopted the habit too.

Dunia has learned how to handle Tatiana and understands that the woman is hungry for love and attention, as most people are. Dunia hums a song as she heads down to breakfast. It's a Christmas song that Zhanna Belovol, the choir director at St. Vladimir's, taught her many years ago. Dunia is trying to remember the words. 'How did that go?' she asks herself. There's an old dusty piano off of the mess hall behind a stack of tools and chairs. Dunia thinks that she could probably sort out some of the harmonies if she could have a little time with it. 'I'm not sure who to ask about that. Do I need permission?' Dunia thinks. The daily grind has relented a bit, now that the harvest is complete. And when the cold weather sets in permanently for the next several months, their tasks will change, perhaps leaving space for a creative project. Dunia has an idea that somehow, with the grace of God, she can teach these women how to sing.

After breakfast, Dunia makes an announcement. "I'm starting a choir. We'll meet on Tuesdays and Thursdays in the afternoon. Anyone that wants to join is welcome. I'll teach you how to sing and harmonize." Some women seem interested while others seem apprehensive or downright bored with Dunia's announcement. "I think we could be quite good," Dunia continues.

"Quite good?" one woman responds doubtfully. "Are we going to sing church songs?"

"Yeah, I don't know if God will approve of a choir full of sluts," Tatiana retorts.

The women laugh and wait for Dunia's response.

Dunia shuffles her feet, "Maybe we could put on a show for Christmas?" This seems to set them alight. The idea of putting on a show buzzes through them. Nobody commits then and there, but the possibility has stirred excitement and by the end of the week, Dunia has ten women signed up.

The next day, the foreman stops Dunia in the hallway as she's headed out to shovel a big dump of snow that's blocking a delivery truck from getting through to the house. "I know about your choir Dunia," he says. Dunia turns and looks at him, her back to the wall. She feels herself bracing for what he might say next. “I know you’re a God loving woman and I respect that,” he pauses and Dunia nods, her face opening up a degree. “I’m ok with it as long as it doesn’t interfere with the work we have to get done around here. We’re building another house this winter and it’s not going to be an easy task for this bunch.”

“Ok,” Dunia replies, “We’ll only meet once the day’s work is completed to your satisfaction.”

“Da da, and you can’t put on a Christmas show. The state rules this place. And the state says that religion cannot exist here,” he says firmly.

The foreman pauses, working something out in his head, “The government sent us this book of Communist songs,” he says, reaching into his coat pocket and pulling out a gray booklet. “They want every person on every collective farm singing these songs. Maybe you could teach them to the women?”

Dunia reluctantly takes the booklet. She looks down and examines the picture. It’s a farm scene where everyone is doing their task with a big satisfied smile on their face. ‘They make communist Russia look like one big happy family,’ she thinks. She’s so angry she could spit.

“Ok,” he says, aware of the tension, “You can sing them to everyone, somewhere toward the end of December.”

Dunia looks up at him, surprised by this detail.

The foreman gives her a sideways glance, turns on his heel and heads back down the hallway toward the kitchen.

A couple days later, Dunia notices that the chairs and tools that had boxed the piano in, have been cleared out. She takes this as the foreman's full support and holds the first official choir rehearsal later that afternoon.

"We sound like balls pounding against an asshole," Medovyy says after they try to sing the first line of the song in harmony. Dunia doesn't disagree but she holds her tongue and turns away from the women to hide her smile.

After a few rehearsals one woman drops out saying, "I'm terrible. I can't carry a tune. I'm sorry but I just can't do this." Dunia knows it's true and watches her walk away with a sense of relief. That same week, she overhears another woman humming to herself as she's mending a hole in her dress. She recognizes the tune. It's a Ukrainian folk song that Maroushka used to sing. Dunia wonders about the woman's roots, where she came from. "You should think about joining the choir," Dunia says, eyebrows raised.

The woman halts her tune immediately. She doesn't respond or even look up from her sewing but smiles to herself as Dunia walks away. Two days later the same woman, Nadiya, shows up for rehearsal with a friend on each arm. They stand in the doorway for a moment before entering and Dunia gives them a nod. And that makes up their choir, twelve women plus Dunia. A curious band of misfits, prostitutes, sluts and criminals lined up in row to sing a communist folk song that none of them believe in.

28

1935: CHRISTMAS

It looks like a bomb went off in Dunia and Tatiana's room. Somehow it became central headquarters for the "Christmas show" and every square inch is occupied in one way or another. Medovvy[61] is sitting on the edge of Tatiana's bed braiding a white ribbon into Nadiya's hair. Nadiya is seated on the floor between Medovvy's legs, reading the lyrics of her solo scrolled onto a scrap of brown parchment paper. Tatiana is using thick red syrup from a jar of cherry preserves to apply color to Vishnya's lips and cheeks. Dresses and skirts are hanging off the door, off the bedpost and off of Tatiana's shoulders as she can never seem to complete one task before moving on to the next. Tatiana and Vishnya are held hostage by a fit of giggles as Tatiana applies the juice to Vishnya's lips and Vishnya promptly licks it off again.

"Goddammit, would you stop that!" Tatiana can barely get the words out or a breath in, she's laughing so hard. The shelf in the corner is draped with underwear, bras, garter belts and stockings. Dunia had wondered how the women acquired such items until she witnessed the delivery boy fucking Medovvy in the supply closet near the back entrance to the kitchen a week ago.

In that moment a week ago, Medovvy's skirts are up around her waist and the boy has his face buried in her hair as he bangs her up against the wall. Dunia is shocked but she doesn't interrupt them. This kind of exchange is not hers to interrupt. She's powerless to stop this particular order of things and she chooses not to interfere. She backs away quietly and stands around the corner listening. She needs to make sure that they're sounds of pleasure or at least feigned pleasure coming from Medovvy's mouth. As Dunia stands there, heart pounding, she thinks about Jacob and the way his eyes used to blaze every time they made love. The experience ignites an ache in Dunia's body. Something she hasn't felt in a long time. Later, she sees Medovvy emerge with a small parcel tucked under her arm. Dunia's sure this isn't an isolated incident.

Later, when she considers it, she realizes she's seen several of the women with contraband; cigarettes, vodka, magazines and the sexy underwear now adorning the wooden shelf in her bedroom. Everyone is getting prepared for the concert. Another choir member stands in the doorway, smoking a cigarette. She's waiting to get her hair braided and her cherry juice make-up done. Four women stand in the hallway practicing harmonies. Their faces are close as they watch each-other's eyes, sensitive to the blend of sound, trying to get it just right. The show begins in half an hour and Dunia has no idea how this chaos is going to come to order in that time. But she's so proud of her little choir. 'Well, we're not St.

Vladimir's choir,' she thinks, taking in the bedroom scene, 'but we're pretty darn good.' Dunia thinks about the time she spent singing with her old friend, Olena, in front of the congregation so many years ago. Her thoughts are interrupted when Nadiya gets up and strips down to change her underwear right there in the middle of the room. Dunia muses, 'What would Zhanna Belovol think if she could see me right now? What would my mother think!?'

Forty minutes later the women shuffle into the mess hall to take the "stage." The audience is made up of the other women that work on the experimental farm, the delivery boy, the foreman and his friend, a soldier that often shows up to stay with the foreman on weekends or at other random times. A high ranking officer from the government has shown up to assess their success with the communist songs. He's standing near the front with pale blue eyes facing forward and a stone cold expression on his face.

"This is a celebration of communist Russia," Dunia hears the foreman say to the officer when he questions the timing of the performance. "We don't have time to practice singing during the summer, or during harvest. This is the perfect time to praise mother Russia." Dunia wipes a drop of sweat from her brow, hoping the officer isn't paying attention too closely to their performance.

In the audience, there are also several families from nearby farms sitting on the supper-bench facing the choir, their backs to the long wooden supper table, which is also partially set for a meal they will all share when the performance is over. Dunia is surprised to see several children in the audience. She worries about the women's behavior and how it might affect them. But she thinks equally that the presence of children might keep them in line and remind them of their own innocent nature. 'These women could actually pass as ladies,' Dunia thinks proudly scanning their faces and taking in the angelic beauty of their hair braided up with white ribbon. Tatiana's extreme cherry rouge gives them away a little bit, but when Dunia doesn't focus on that, she could almost see this choir performing at St. Vladimir's. For a minute, Dunia closes her eyes and pictures them there, the sun streaming in through stained glass windows casting warm light onto their faces, the smell of spring lilacs pouring in from the open doors and bird-song twittering in from a nest in the massive oak tree on the church lawn. She sees Nepefan and Maroushka there too, sitting in the pews awaiting their performance. Dunia's eyes are wet when she opens them again. She takes a deep breath, turns toward the audience and introduces their first song.

The celebration goes well past midnight. The officer leaves shortly after the performance is over saying something about catching an early train. Everyone feasts on the *Celebration of Mother Russia* spread. Several of the women were put in charge of the menu and the table is now lined with the crumbs of braided bread and cherry tarts. The empty dishes reveal remnants of chicken stew and a pork sausage seasoned with garlic and paprika, a contribution brought by one of the neighbors. The remains of a root vegetable salad made of beets, carrots and apples chopped finely together are swimming in the final dregs of a vinaigrette dressing.

Dunia has begun to tidy up, eating her way through the last of the food as she moves along the table. The neighbors have mostly gone now, children reluctantly surrendering to the will of their parents and their own tiredness after such a busy day together. The neighbors have long slogs through the snowy fields to get back to their homes and the warmth of their own beds. Tatiana is still carrying on, stealing nips from a flask of vodka she's been hiding in the pocket of her dress and flirting with the delivery boy. Dunia is certain that the boy will be satisfied tonight, but not without a price. Tatiana is a natural flirt and loves to play, but she's out for business and never gives it away without payment. 'Everyone here is surviving in one way or another,' Dunia thinks, as she scrapes and spoons the last of the chicken stew into her mouth.

Dunia carries the dishes into the kitchen and pauses when she hears heavy breathing coming from the supply closet. 'Don't these people have beds?' she thinks as she rounds the corner. As her eyes adjust, she's stunned to see the foreman and his soldier friend locked in an embrace. She hurries out of the kitchen quietly wondering, 'Why am I always walking in on people? Are people just screwing each other all the time around here?' Dunia doesn't know what to do with what she's witnessed. That night she tosses and turns thinking about it, trying to make sense of this thing she's never known. Tatiana finally squeezes the truth out of her the following morning after witnessing Dunia wringing her hands and pacing for an hour.

"Yeah yeah, we all know that already." Tatiana says waving it away like it's nothing. "We kind of got a clue when he didn't want to fuck any of us."

Dunia sits on the edge of her bed staring down at her hands, shocked by what Tatiana's saying.

"People love each other in different ways, Dunia. You're not in the village anymore. And some of us don't care what the church has to say about us." Tatiana sits down on the bed next to Dunia, "The foreman is a good man, I might be alive because of him and that's all I care about."

"Anyways, the celebration was a success!" Tatiana says, putting her arm around Dunia and smiling brightly. "The officer was too busy rearranging the pickle up his ass to notice that we changed the lyrics to his shitty songs."

29

THE WIND SHIFTS

Dunia wakes up suddenly. The room is still dark, though a sliver of light from the window whispers "early morning." Something shakes her awake, a sound. There it is again. Dunia can hear men's voices coming from down the hall. "Wake up!" They are shouting, opening doors and turning on lights as they go. They are making their way down the hallway. An officer bursts through her bedroom door and flicks on the light. "Wake up!" he shouts. Dunia looks at him stunned. "It's time to go," he says, "You have five minutes to be ready and at the front door." Dunia has no idea what's happening but she starts gathering her clothing in a frenzy, grabbing a small satchel from underneath her bed. Tatiana is equally lost and confused, running around and gathering items onto a piece of green cloth she has laid out on her bed.

Barely a minute goes by and the officer is back, banging a baton against the wall saying "Move, move, move." Dunia stumbles out the door and down to the front room. Here, she sees the women, her friends and family over the past two years, gathered in various states of disarray. The foreman stands at the back of the room, his face is pale and he is staring straight ahead. He refuses to make eye contact with Dunia. Vishnya is still in her night-gown, her hands are clasped to her chest and her hair is a mass of blond tangles. Others are dressed and carrying small bags of clothing or other items. Medovvy is clutching a picture of a child in a small silver frame. One woman is leaning into Tatiana and softly weeping on her shoulder. We are all awaiting the next instruction.

The guards, men that Dunia has never seen before, begin separating the women into three groups.

"You here," he says, pointing to Medovvy and then to a spot on the floor near the front window.

"And you, over here!" he says to Tatiana, pointing her to a space toward the back nearer to the kitchen.

It is then that Dunia sees the same government officer that attended their Christmas show - the one with the cold blue eyes. He is looking at a list of names and discussing something with one of the guards. He seems to be in charge.

When the women have been divided, two of the groups are loaded onto separate trucks that are growling outside on the driveway. Dunia is among them and she notices the same driver that brought her here, watching them from his driver-side window, as they make their way out the door. His expression is darker than the last time she saw him. If it wasn't for his hat, she may not have recognized him at all. The group that Dunia moves with, bottlenecks at the tailgate of the truck, where the disoriented prisoners are doing their best to hoist themselves up onto the flat bed as quickly as they can. The force of the guards moves them into place and scatters their minds at the same time. Dunia finds it impossible to focus. It's as if her mind has cracked into pieces.

Dunia notices then that the third group of women seem to be staying on the farm. She can't determine what led the men to put one woman here and another woman there. There is no obvious pattern. This makes it all the more frustrating. She wants to know what's happening as much as the next woman, but the officers tell them nothing. Dunia looks back into the front window of the house and sees Tatiana staring out. Her fingers are touching the glass lightly and her eyes are wide, searching for Dunia. Dunia gazes back and at last they make eye contact. They share a moment like this before the truck lurches forward and barrels off down the drive and out toward the wide world and to God knows where. Dunia holds her bundle to herself. She smells the fabric of her clothing. She can smell the house in her clothing. It smells like wood smoke and cherries and Tatiana's contraband perfume. Dunia weeps.

The truck bumps down a gravel road just as the sun starts peeking up over the horizon. After a time, they come to a junction. The two trucks that have been traveling together for the past hour, separate here. One truck turns left on the highway heading back up toward Moscow. The truck Dunia rides in turns right and heads south. Dunia feels a spark of hope. Her home is south of here. 'Could this be over soon?' she thinks. The road is smooth and paved. Dunia ties a scarf around her head to block the cool morning breeze. Her eyes are dry now and she stares out at the landscape. 'God, where are you taking me now? Be gentle with me. I want to go home.'

They travel all morning, stopping only once to fuel up and go to the bathroom. The sun is high in the sky when they arrive in Voronezh and Dunia and the others are loaded onto a train. She sits in the corner of the train car scanning the faces of the people around her, looking for someone she might know. She sees a young mother seated in one corner with a little girl seated between her legs. The little girl is holding a well-loved stuffed rabbit and has a smudge of dirt across her cheek. Dunia sees a teenage boy. He reminds her of Ivan, her own son. She wonders where his mother is. The train sits idle for the better part of an hour, when at last a shrill whistle announces its imminent departure. The train chugs south southeast. Dunia watches the light shining in through the high train-car window. They travel for several hours. She can't seem to slow her heart or settle her nerves. She's waiting for the next shout, the next push, the next order. At last the train slows and comes to a stop. The train car is wrenched open.

"It's time to go," one of the guards shouts from the platform. Dunia's really tired of hearing him say that.

The guards herd them through the streets pressing the muzzle of their rifles into the prisoner's backs to keep them moving. 'There are only four guards here,' Dunia thinks, 'If each of us ran in different directions, some of us would get away.' But they aren't organized. Dunia is having a hard time organizing her own thoughts after this morning's traumatic awakening.

The road leads them through an industrial area and down a steep hill towards the port. There, a ship awaits them. A prisoner leans in and whispers into Dunia's ear. She feels repulsed by the man's sour breath. He's missing several teeth and she thinks he might be mad. "We're going to need bottles for water," he says pointing sharply toward a crate full of glass bottles tucked behind an oily coil of rope.

"You there!" a guard shouts at him, "Shut up!" Dunia doesn't understand the man's message but something inside her tells her to pay attention. She snatches two of the bottles and tucks them into her satchel.

Next, they're loaded onto the boat, single file across a wooden plank. As the horn blares and the ship pulls away from port, Dunia wonders, 'Will I ever see this shore again?' She stands there, watching the gritty, gray buildings recede into the distance. The sun is beginning to dip down in the sky. She stands there for a long time watching as it disappears over the horizon. As far as she looks in any direction now, all she can see is the dark blue water rising and falling.

At last she surrenders her watch, surrenders her need to know what comes next, surrenders her grip. She sits down with her meager bundle of belongings and rests quietly. She's surprised by how calm she is. 'I could be dead tomorrow,' she thinks. And in a strange way, the thought soothes her. Soon the gentle rocking of the ship lulls her into a deep sleep. By the time she awakens the next day, the sun is high in the sky. Dunia squints and shields her eyes from the light. She looks around. The people look rough and tired. They are unwashed and lost, just as she is, with grim expressions on their faces. Dunia sees an old man squat down over a bucket and take a shit right out in the open. She turns away and moves to the edge of the ship. She watches the waves. She stares out at the dark churning sea. Her eyes are lost in the swirling eddies of foamy water.

For three nights and two days they roll across the sea. They are offered a watery soup at one point and many of the passengers struggle to keep it down. The bump and sway of the ship has brought several to their knees. And yet, sea-sick and exhausted as they are, Dunia is touched by the kindness she witnesses among them; a young man giving up his blanket for a sea-sick old lady and a burly man lifting up a small child so she can watch the ocean waves slapping against the side of the ship.

At last, near the end of the second day. The guards begin shouting and organizing them. Something is happening. "Fill up your bottles here!" one of the guards shouts, pointing to an enormous water barrel with a metal spout. "You're going to need it," he says, laughing towards another guard.

Dunia lines up and fills her bottles thinking, 'I don't understand what could be funny about this.' Afterward, she moves to the edge of the ship and sees that the ship is approaching an island. There is a mob of people gathered on the shore. They are huddled up together. They're screaming something and as the ship moves closer, Dunia strains to hear. The roar of surf muffles the sound of their shrieks. White gulls are circling and crying out from above. As they move into earshot, Dunia realizes the people are calling out for water. "Water, water!" They say, "We're dying of thirst!"

30

1936: THE ISLAND OF PRORVA

The ship approaches its mooring along a crude wooden dock built out into the bay of the island of Prorva[1]. The sun shines through light pink, feathered clouds and a warm fragrant breeze blows in off of the Azov Sea. Four armed guards stand at the bow, ready to fasten the ship as she creaks and groans, moving slowly into place.

"These fools have no idea that there's no fresh water on this island," one guard says to another. He's stocky and solid with a weathered face and an angry red scar across his eyebrow.

"Well…they're about to find out!" the other guard responds with a laugh. He has dark curly hair and Dunia sees a gap between his front teeth when he laughs. If the circumstances were different, she may have described him as handsome.

"What about the natives?" Scar guard asks.

1. Abyss

"They're threatened with death if they are caught helping in any way," the other responds, "They're peaceful. They have children… families… they're not going to jeopardize that."

The conversation is lost in a flurry of activity. The ship shifts into place and the guard's spring into action, attaching several thick bow lines to large metal cleats on the dock. Next they carry a thick wooden plank and lay it down as a bridge over the water. The prisoners are corralled forward toward the dock by the guards in the rear of the ship that have now finished attaching the stern lines. Several guards jump off of the ship ahead of them and line the dock with their rifles aimed toward land.

Dunia sees the prisoners on the island moving like a wave toward the dock, looking desperately toward the ship. Dunia sees a woman with a tattered skirt and blood stained knees run out toward them. Halfway along the dock, she sways and falls. She is shouting something in Ukrainian. Dunia strains to listen but the woman's words don't make sense. She's delirious with thirst. Gap-toothed guard throws his head back, laughing at her.

"I'm sorry, we can't understand you," he says in mock sympathy.

Suddenly, Dunia feels the weight of the water bottles in her satchel and feels afraid. She fears not having water to drink, as much as she fears being attacked or killed for the water she does have. 'How am I going to get past these prisoners?' she thinks.

The guards escort them out of the ship and march them along the dock toward the island. As she gets closer to land, she can see the prisoner's grubby faces. The crowd on land, eyes those disembarking, with a look so ravenous that Dunia instinctively moves left, putting a man with a thick brown beard and enormous hands between her and the horde. There's tension. There's electricity in the air. The crowd is waiting for an inborn signal, to descend and devour.

Bang bang bang! One of the guards fires up into the air. The throng sprawls backwards, screaming and shouting. In the chaos of this moment, Dunia steps off the dock and follows her instincts. She moves left, walking swiftly along the rocky beach. Her eyes are on the ground as she steps carefully to avoid the gaping tide-pools. The beach curves around a rocky outcropping, and here Dunia begins to climb up a craggy slope. Her heart is pounding, but another force is moving her now. She refuses to look back, as if her gaze will break whatever spell is protecting her from view. She's unstoppable. When she reaches the safety of the trees, she finally turns back and looks. Madness has overtaken the beach. The guards have pulled back toward the ship and a battle has broken out among the prisoners. Dunia continues to watch the mayhem until she sees one man smash another man's head open with a rock. His blood and brains spill out all over the mossy stones along the shoreline. Dunia is holding onto the trunk of a vast cedar tree and notices that she has inadvertently dug her fingernails into the strings of its bark. She steps back. She breathes.

They are all prisoners now and in a few days they will blend into one desperate mass. Dunia will not be among them. She knows her life depends on getting away from this shore. She reaches into her satchel and pulls out a bottle. She examines the water through the glass. She pulls out the cork and takes a sip. It's cool and sweet in her mouth. She has never understood its value more acutely than she does right now.

She gathers herself together and starts moving inland through the brush. She moves as quietly as she can, looking left and right, scanning the landscape for any movement. The sun is going down now and she figures she has an hour before the land will be lost in shadows. For some reason, as she walks along, she thinks of a bed-time story Maroushka used to tell her. It was the tale of a little girl with flowers growing in her hair. She lived in the forest and slept in the hollow of a tree every night.

"Maybe I could sleep in a tree," Dunia says to herself. And then she laughs at the thought. She has formed an image of herself coiled up inside the base of a hollow tree and it strikes her funny. Laughter bubbles and boils out of her. She can't stop. Her body is wracked with it. She leans up against a big gray stone, trying to gain control of herself. It seems that she's been taken over. She's brought down to her knees, hysterical. Then her laughter breaks and turns into something else. Deep guttural sobs. Dunia barely escaped with her life today. She saw her comrades ripped apart. She braces herself against the rock. Her body is shaking and trembling. She lets it happen. She can't fight her own being. She feels everything that she's been holding together over the last few days; the loss of the experimental farm and her family there, the loss of her choir and Tatiana. "She was my sister," Dunia says angrily, "Why do you take everything away from me!?" Dunia lays down on the ground and continues to shake and twitch, calling out to God, "Now what God! Now what!" As the land grows dark, Dunia's body begins to relax and calm. She sits up and looks inside her satchel. She takes a drink of water and looks out at the land which is already shrouded in twilight. The water tastes like life. What she has will not last long, perhaps a couple of days. Next, Dunia puts on all of her clothes and wraps a scarf around her head. She sits down and leans her back against the stone. It feels warm, still radiating heat from the sun.

'An island with no fresh water,' Dunia thinks, turning the guards' words over in her mind. "I didn't know such a place existed," she says out loud, the sounds of her own voice bringing her back into the moment, its echo reminding her that she's still alive.

"Ok God, you crazy son of a bitch, what's next?"

31

WATER

Dunia refuses to believe that the island has no fresh water. "That can't be right," she says to herself as she steps over a prodigious fallen log with orange and green lichen growing in circular patches along its flank. The morning sun is pouring sideways through the trees and songbirds flit back and forth, snatching insects out of the air. A dark brown squirrel races up a cedar tree and looks back at her, releasing his "fierce" warning call. He is less intimidating than he thinks. Dunia smiles at the sight of him and follows his progress through the trees. His tail flips back and forth like it has a mind of its own. When he's satisfied with his dominance in the situation, he races further up the tree and retrieves a nut. Then he holds it between his paws and gnaws it in a frenzy. All the while, he keeps his dark beady eyes focused on Dunia, as if to say, "This is my nut! Watch helplessly as I devour it!!"

Dunia wonders if there are nuts she could harvest out of these trees. Food has not been a problem so far. Dunia found a patch of blueberries and wild sorrel first thing this morning. The berries were sun ripened in low bushes. She found them right on the other side of the boulder she had slept beside, the night before. On the path ahead of her, she notices a cluster of Shaggy Mane mushrooms. She wanders over and bends down to gather them up. Today, she's determined to find water. A stream, a spring, there must be something. Dunia has one bottle of water left. But with the temperature rising and the effort of her journey, she'll need to drink again soon. She hugs her satchel to herself.

The path veers left and after a while Dunia finds herself walking along a high cliff jutting out over a rocky shoreline. Dunia looks down over the edge and sees that the beach is deserted. 'If I can see a path that leads me down there, I'll follow it. There might be crabs or other shellfish to eat down there.' She imagines a beautiful freshet flowing down the side of the cliff. It seems possible. Dunia stops and drinks from her second bottle. It's almost halfway gone now. She holds its contents up to the light. She's been doing this a lot, as if her constant, vigilant attention will slow the depletion of her water supply. As Dunia walks further, the rough craggy cliff softens and tapers off into a steep sand dune with tufts of marram grass. Here she begins her descent toward the beach.

Large blue-black boulders line the shore and Dunia hops and steps carefully toward the water. She squats down to examine the contents of a big green tide pool. She sees tiny fish and hermit crabs. The rocks here are covered in crusty, cream colored barnacles. Dunia stands closer to the water and looks back at the cliff. She scans its surface for fresh flowing water. The cliff face is dry. Where the cliff meets the sea, Dunia sees purple and orange sea-stars clinging to the rocks. The sea is calm. Dunia takes off her shoes and steps into the water. It's warm. Dunia can see fish swimming all around. The water is thick with them. 'Food is not going to be a problem.' The fish are so plentiful Dunia thinks that she might be able to scoop one out of the water with her bare hands.

Dunia hears a sound in the distance and peers down the beach. It sounds like children's laughter. She scans the sky, the rocks and the water lapping and curling toward the shore. Then, suddenly, a child steps out of the woods. Dunia gasps and falls to the ground, her skirts dipping into the tide pool. She stays low and moves back onto the shore, hiding behind a smooth gray stone. She peers around the rock and continues to watch, entranced. It's a little boy wearing a brown robe and a round cap on his head. Dunia squints, unsure if she's seeing this. A little girl comes racing on his heels, skipping from rock to rock and calling after the boy. The wind whips her dark curly hair back and forth and a green scarf trails out behind her like a flag. Dunia continues to stare, the scene so surreal, she struggles to fathom it. Then several women and men step out of the woods and onto the beach. Dunia's heart pounds as she observes from her hiding place. The women wear scarves over their heads and long flowing robes. Their clothing waves and ripples in the breeze. The men are dressed in long shirts and loose fitting pants. Some of them wear hats on their heads or have their heads wrapped up in cloth. Dunia can see large scythes hanging down at the men's hips. 'Yes,' Dunia thinks, 'I would wear a knife at my hip if I lived on this island too.'

Dunia sits and breathes, gathering her thoughts. 'These must be the natives,' Dunia thinks. 'Well, what do they drink? How are they living here?' She settles herself behind the rock, peering out to spy on the strangers. She's made a decision that she's going to follow them and find out how they live.

The men cast a net into the water and pull it back in. It comes back to them moving and wriggling and Dunia can see the wet flash of silver. The men put the fish into a pail and release several of the smaller ones back into the water. Meanwhile, the women have built a fire on the beach. The children are closer to Dunia now, squatting down looking at something between the rocks. 'A tide-pool filled with mysterious creatures.' Dunia thinks.

The family cooks their meal over the fire and one of the women calls out to the children. She speaks in a language Dunia doesn't recognize. The words sound thick and sensual with a distinctive rolling of the r's. She assumes that the mother is calling her children to lunch. Dunia's stomach rumbles. She takes another drink of her water. Her body is sore from crouching on the rocks. She's grateful the stone is shielding her from the heat of the sun. Dunia watches a little brown crab crawling from the water, past her spot near the rock and toward a teeming pool of water to her left. The critter is unaware of Dunia until he gets close and the flap of her dress alerts him. He raises his pinchers up in the air and continues moving sideways, in his defensive posture, toward his destination. 'Everyone is trying to stay alive.'

Dunia sits and waits for several hours before the family begins gathering itself up and heading back in the direction from which they came. She waits until they're out of sight and then begins to follow them. She struggles to walk, as her legs have fallen asleep sitting on the ground for so long. She moves as quickly as she can, afraid of losing her life-line. Dunia follows their path up into the trees. She can't decide which way they've gone. The little girl squeals in the distance, offering Dunia her next clue. She follows the sound and finds herself walking along a narrow dirt pathway. She's lost sight of them now and doesn't hear another sound. But she continues walking, trusting the path to lead her.

32

THE NATIVES

The sun is going down and Dunia rounds a bend in the path. She climbs a hillside, painted purple by the fading light and stands at its crest, catching her breath. When she gazes in the distance a big, round, orange moon is staring back at her. It takes her breath away. For a moment she can't fathom the size of it. It's immense and glorious, sitting low on the horizon. Dunia sits on the grass and drinks the last of her water. She keeps her eyes on the sky and wonders if anyone she loves is sharing this moment with the moon, miles and miles away from the Island of Prorva. She thinks about Jacob and about her children. She can feel that Jacob is with her now and maybe Mary too. How could such a vulnerable little child survive all of this madness? She thinks about her mother and Maroushka. She pictures them safe at home baking bread in the piche, while her father is outside chopping wood and stacking it in a neat pile against the side of the hut. Of course she knows that this vision is only a dream, but it brings her comfort. She thinks about the official and wonders if he's still alive. "Is he still fighting his sickness?" Dunia asks out loud. She is speaking her thoughts out loud more and more, voicing her inner world to the trees. And she thinks about Tatiana. She knows Tatiana is still alive. She can feel her fighting spirit. She's a survivor. Like Dunia.

Dunia lays back on the earth. She's hungry. Her stomach feels hollow. She needs to eat meat. She needs to make a fire somehow. And if she doesn't find water soon, she'll be dead anyway. But right now, she's bone tired. So she closes her eyes and sleeps.

She wakes up in the early morning shaking with cold. A dew has settled on her clothes making everything damp. The moon has moved across the sky but is still there, staring down at her with a blue-white ethereal glow. "My clothing is damp!" Dunia says. She looks around and sees the sparkle of dew decorating each blade of grass. She gets down on her knees and collects the drops on her tongue. There are low bushes to her right and the tip of each leaf contains its own life-giving drop. Dunia gathers these up on her tongue too. Then, in spite of the chill, Dunia takes off her dress and her scarf and lays them out on the grass to collect the moisture. For the next hour she performs this process several times over, laying her clothing on the wet ground and wringing the moisture out into one of her bottles. It's tedious and slow going. "I'll do whatever I have to do to stay alive," she says to herself and to the hill and to the moon. As the morning brightens with the rising sun, Dunia has filled one of her bottles up to the halfway point. The water is a murky gray. Dunia drinks. In spite of the dust and the grit, it tastes like heaven.

"That's one way to do the laundry," Dunia says, throwing her head back and laughing. She's giddy about the water. It allows her one more day out here. She wonders how bizarre she must look right now, standing in her underwear and gathering dew drops. She imagines that Jacob can see her now and takes pleasure in it.

Suddenly Dunia stops. She smells something. Woodsmoke. "The Natives," Dunia whispers. She follows the smell to the brow of the hill and looks downward. There, at the base of the trees, she sees the glow of a fire. As her eyes adjust, she sees that the fire is surrounded by strange circular huts with softly pointed roofs. She's never seen homes quite like these before. They're covered in cloth or animal hide. Each one has a little chimney and several of them have smoke curling skyward. Dunia hears the bleat of a goat. She crouches down instinctively. Then she notices that she's still in her underwear and suddenly she feels vulnerable. She backs away from the spot and returns to her clothing. She dresses. She shivers with the shock of her cold wet dress, but also with the excitement of having discovered the village. Today, she'll observe them and find out how they live.

Dunia gathers herself together and returns to the edge of the hill. The direct path downward is steep and muddy and she decides to backtrack a little ways and go around instead. The sun is shining brightly now and Dunia notices that her dress is steaming. She holds out her arm to watch the steam rising. She's grateful for the warmth of the day. She follows the path back down the way she came and then loses it again in the trees. After searching for a path leading toward the village for several minutes, Dunia becomes frustrated and simply turns herself in its direction and heads straight through the bush. She steps over a jumbled tangle of bushes and her foot lands on a dry stick, letting out a *crack*. Dunia stops and puts her hand to her mouth, aware of her carelessness. "You need to be quiet," Dunia whispers, looking down at the deadwood "Just calm down and go slow."

When Dunia looks up again, a man is standing at the edge of the clearing watching her. Dunia startles and gasps, hand on her heart. The man doesn't react but continues to watch her with an equal measure of calm and curiosity. His skin is dark and he wears a cream-coloured cloth wrapped around his head. He's dressed in a long robe-like shirt and loose fitting pants. Dunia is aware of the massive knife hanging by his side. He is beautiful and exotic. But the part that stands out the most, are his eyes. They are light amber. And as he watches her steadily, Dunia can only describe what she sees in them, as kindness. Dunia smiles at him. He doesn't smile back, but Dunia's aware of a softening in the energy between them. She imagines that he's a father.

"Please," Dunia says, "I need water."

The man doesn't respond and Dunia knows he probably doesn't understand.

She reaches into her bag and the man takes a step back.

"No, please, please," Dunia pleads, showing him one of her bottles, "water, I need water."

Now she sees recognition in his eyes. But she watches his expression go from open to closed in an instant.

"Hayir[1]!" he says firmly, shaking his head and taking another step back.

Then he speaks in his language. Dunia doesn't understand his words but his gesture is clear. He's asking her to leave. To go back the way she came.

"Please," Dunia says, "I'll die if I don't find water. Where do you get your water?"

Of course he can't understand her, Dunia knows this but she can't stop the flow of words. She has to get through to this man and she feels like she could. He has a heart. But Dunia also remembers what she heard the guard say - that the natives are threatened with death and death to their families if they assist the prisoners in any way.

Dunia understands his position.

The man draws his knife now and continues asking her to leave in his thick, smoky language. He's getting louder now and Dunia fears it might draw others from the village to his side.

She steps back. She feels defeated. This was her only hope. Her eyes prickle and fill with tears but don't spill over. They stand there looking at each other like this. Each one is equally aware of the other's needs, and is poised, waiting to see what the other will do next. The moment feels primal. At last, Dunia backs down, turns and heads down the path in the direction from which she came.

1. No (In Turkish)

33

DEATH

Dunia walks back through the forest. She isn't following any set path now. She is just walking-walking wherever her legs decide to take her. She feels dejected and lost. She has wandered the whole morning and now, as the heat of the afternoon sun presses down on the island, the forest remains cool. A sanctuary. A church. The house of God. Dunia drops to her knees. The earth is soft and gives way. Time has slowed down. She has nowhere to go, nowhere to be and nothing to do. Her hope was so wrapped up in the natives that, in its absence, she feels a gaping void. It was ripped from her hand. It slipped through her fingers like water. Water! "I don't know if I'm going to make it," Dunia says, the words rippling back in her mind after leaving her lips - back and forth, back and forth back and forth like waves. She feels like she's in a dream. She looks out through the trees. A mist hangs in the air, creating softness around the plants and softness to the light. It only adds to the surreal quality of the afternoon. Dunia drinks the last sip of her "dew" water. She's been hanging onto it as long as she can. But she is beyond thirsty now. She sees that the forest is offering food; berries, greens, nuts, mushrooms, but the desire to eat has disappeared. She needs one thing - water. 'How did I fall so far, so fast?' Dunia wonders.

In the distance, Dunia hears the surf. The rush, the white caps, the foam of the sea and she feels drawn to it. 'Maybe I'll lie down next to the water,' she thinks. She hoists herself up and heads straight through the trees, toward the sound. Dunia steps out onto a rocky beach and into the sun. It blazes down on her and she shields her eyes. She doesn't want to hide from the light anymore. "Come and find me now," Dunia says out loud. She is speaking to the soldiers and perhaps to God. She's not worried about the sun leaching the moisture from her body, or the soldiers shooting her dead. She feels that the end is near. She walks across the rocks. She stumbles, regains her balance and makes her way to the water's edge. She's so tempted to drink. She knows it would only make her sick. But her craving for water defies all logic. In the gentle waves, she feels the draw of death. It's not violent but gently lapping, peaceful and steady. 'How did I come to the precipice so quickly?' she thinks. "I wanted more time," she says out loud, through parched lips.

She makes her way down to a big flat rock near the shore and lies down. 'I'll make this my bed,' she thinks. She turns onto her side and watches the waves lapping gently at the shore. The water is in constant motion and it mesmerizes. The waves are green and coming in at various angles now bumping into each other and changing course. The sun is burning her cheek but she hardly feels it. She feels herself slipping into nothing and it's calling her. Inviting her to surrender. She has been fighting for so long; following this path, fighting to stay alive. And maybe now it's time to rest; to let go of the fight, to submit. If this is it, she's ready to go quietly; peacefully. Dunia sleeps. And dreams.

Dunia is walking in a dry creek-bed near her parent's hut in Kobeliaky. It's spring and the field is painted in the brilliant colors of wildflowers; blue, magenta and indigo. There are bright yellow sunflowers lining a fence in the distance. Dunia sees a path and follows it down to a deep blue lake. She's never been here before and wonders how she missed this place. The lake is almost a perfect circle and Dunia knows that its depth is endless. She walks to the water's edge, bends down and drinks. She looks into the water and feels that she could dive right in. She knows an underwater world awaits her there. She sees something shining in the hidden depths of the water, calling to her. As the ripples on the water still, she sees her own reflection and watches it transform. She sees a glimmer of Maroushka's face and then it morphs into Jacob's face and then into the face of Jesus and finally back to her own face. Suddenly she hears the call of a strange bird. It's calling from the direction of the hut. There it is again. It doesn't sound like any bird Dunia has ever known. The sound occupies her head now and it is pulling her away, away, away from the lake and up and out of the dream.

Dunia is laying on the rock and her face is pressed into the stone. The sun is setting in the distance. The clouds are lit up in orange, pink and lavender before her. At first she can only see sky. 'Am I in heaven?' she wonders. The colors of sky and sea have bled into one. It takes a moment for Dunia to find the line of distinction between them. Again she hears the strange bird-call from her dream. It's coming from the water. Dunia lifts her head and looks closely. Something is moving out in the surf, darting this way and that way, cutting through the water. There's another one. What is it? Dunia can see two of them moving around in the water. Darting back and forth, splashing and then coming up for air. They are squealing and clicking. Sending strange tones back and forth to one another. 'They're speaking,' Dunia thinks, transfixed by their strange language. She's only ever heard about dolphins. And she always wondered if they were fantasy. 'Is this real? Am I here?' she asks. She sits up and wraps her arms around her legs, watching, listening. 'Are they hunting?' Dunia wonders. One dolphin swims in circles around the other, squealing and moaning. Then the creature dives down and shoots out of the water. It lands on its back sending a spray of water in all directions. The other dolphin responds to this display in what Dunia can only describe as laughter. 'I think they're playing,' Dunia thinks. "Here I am facing the end of the world and these creatures are playing," Dunia says out loud, surprised by the strength of her own voice. Suddenly she realizes that the creatures have heard her. They've changed the way they move and one of them has its eye above the water. He's looking at her. Dunia stares back. "You can see me!" she says. And Dunia knows that she's still alive. Suddenly her body revolts, she retches, bringing up the meager contents of her stomach. She's on her feet now. She feels the stone beneath her. She wobbles. She regains her balance.

The cool of the evening air refreshes her. The dolphins continue to swim and play in the cove. Dunia walks back across the stones, back to the woods, back to the path and toward the native's village.

34

KHAZARS

Pronounced (Kah-zar-z): A Turkish tribe of semi-nomadic people

The forest is bathed in the cool blue tones of twilight. Dunia steps out from behind a grove of trees and moves toward the village. She can feel the exact moment that she crosses territorial lines. Her gut registers an invisible sphere surrounding the wide elongated circle of huts. Her instincts are sharp. She knows she risks her life with this action. But her life is over without it. She remembers the Native's warning. She can see the intensity of the man's amber eyes as he sent her away. She wants to respect him and his position but her desperation surpasses all boundaries. And God has led her here. She needs help if she's going to survive. Survival operates on its own unique set of laws; life above all else. She feels calm and steady as she walks toward the clearing. Her stomach is empty and her body is beyond thirsty, to the point that it feels unusually calm and quiet. No gurgle in her stomach, no movement in her gut, just the strong and steady beat of her heart echoing through the hollow of her belly. The pulse urges her forward.

Dunia peers out from behind a hut. There is a soft glow from the central fire-pit and a small gathering of villagers. One woman stirs the contents of a steaming pot resting in the coals. A group of men stand nearby, one of them sharing what seems to be a lively story. He gestures wildly and at a particular moment of exuberance, the group erupts in a rumble of laughter. The woman chimes in, making a short statement that elevates the laughter to a new height. Dunia can feel their good nature. She takes joy in their joy, even though she can't understand the joke. Life has boiled down to the basics for Dunia and she knows what matters. These connections, family and friendship, are everything. She longs to be a part of it. These could be her brothers and sisters.

Just then, a woman with a red scarf around her shoulders, steps out from the hut beside her. She's carrying a small boy on her hip and looking out toward the fire-pit clicking her tongue. The boy says something to his mother and wriggles around, trying to free himself from her arms. The moment she sets him down he's running. He runs outward in a wide arch and stops dead when he sees Dunia pressed against his neighbor's hut. He calls out to his mother who shouts a warning to the villagers around the fire. And in what feels like an instant, Dunia has been hauled out of her hiding place and into the light of the central fire-pit. She stands at their mercy, dizzy and exhausted, hands held up and open in front of her.

The men say things to her. She senses they are asking her questions, pointing this way and that, shrugging their shoulders. Of course, Dunia can't understand or respond in their language but she responds in hers, keeping her voice calm, steady and quiet. The woman that was cooking her meal, packs up what she has and slips away, returning quietly to her hut. Dunia has a sense that the woman is "washing her hands of Dunia," afraid to become involved in politics that could lead to her own death or the death of her family. These are good people, Dunia can see that. But they're afraid that helping an outsider, a prisoner, could lead to their own death. Dunia stands still, listening. A feeling that she is awaiting her sentence washes over her. The men continue talking to each other, arguing their points back and forth, gesturing towards Dunia now and then. Dunia's life over the past six years has been a trial. She's used to it. She stands and waits. The conversation goes on. Dunia feels unsteady and she begins to sway. As the noise of the argument continues, other men leave their huts and come and join in the exchange. One of them is the man with the amber eyes. Dunia makes eye contact with him briefly before the darkness begins to close in around her. Now the sound is muffled, her knees buckle and she falls to the ground. Dunia's world goes black.

35

GOD

Dunia becomes aware of her body. She drifts into consciousness. She feels something against her lips. A wet cloth. Water drips gently into her mouth. She drinks. Her body drinks. It knows what to do all on its own. And she observes it. Then she sinks back into the warm dark abyss. It's so quiet there; quiet and peaceful. She knows that she's alive. She can feel the warm pulse of blood through her veins. But she doesn't have the strength to move or even to open her eyes. Her body is heavy. Her eye-lids are heavy. She's stuck in molasses. It's delicious. She hears the voice of a man. He's speaking words that Dunia doesn't understand. She feels the rhythm of his voice, the deep, warm texture of his words. They comfort her. She can sense the goodness of this man. The sound drifts away and the darkness swallows her again. She stays there, floating in it. Floating in absolute stillness, save the steady rhythm of her heart. Suddenly there is laughter. It bubbles up, rising and falling all around her. It sounds like a song. Dunia hears the voices of children. They're playing. One child is shouting to the other. It's pure joy! Dunia holds the feeling and it wraps itself around her heart. Then the weight, the heaviness pulls her downward once again, into oblivion. Time goes by. It has no meaning. Dunia is lost in a beautiful, shimmering moment. She can feel the presence of God holding her, keeping her safe. She hears the man's voice again, calm and steady, reciting those words. The steady stream of words ripples over her, like water. She knows she is safe, warm and dry. But she's too heavy to fight her weakness and she drops again down, down, down into the void. She is connected to everything that exists in this moment; the void, the voice and those words flowing all around her, anchoring her to this place.

Time passes. Dunia passes in and out of her dark world. She has no idea where she is or how long she's been there.

At last, Dunia finds the strength to move. It begins with the voice of a child. She can feel his breath on her cheek. She can sense that he is very close now, looking at her. Her eyes flutter and then open. She looks up and tries to understand the faces that are looking back down at her. The boy turns his head and calls out to someone else in the room. The girl simply stares. Her hand is resting softly on Dunia's arm. Dunia can feel the warmth of it. The girl is wearing a green scarf around her head. Thick dark curls peek out from one side of the scarf and spill over her shoulder. The girl lifts the scarf over her mouth and bats her eyelashes. Dunia smiles. She wants to laugh but she doesn't have the strength. The girl squeals and runs off, out of Dunia's view. Dunia is too weak to follow the movement. Anything outside of her immediate view is hard to grasp. Dunia can only see what's directly in front of her. The boy returns carrying a wet cloth. He reaches out and holds it to Dunia's lips. It's so saturated with water that it drips down Dunia's chin and onto the soft blanket that's covering her. Dunia slurps. The water is so sweet, so fresh and so delicious.

Then the mother steps into Dunia's field of vision and takes over the task, clicking her tongue at the boy and wringing some of the water out into a basin. The mother feels kind and fierce, a force to be reckoned with. Dunia feels held by her presence. Sunlight is now streaming into the room casting light onto a shelf lined with bowls and gourds. A stunning tapestry of a pastoral scene hangs on the wall and Dunia wonders how such colors were derived from nature. The boy shouts something and breaks into laughter as he skips out the door and into the blinding sunlight. Dunia can hear his voice receding into the distance. The mother says something to her. Dunia doesn't understand the language but feels the intention – to soothe, to calm, to hold safe. Then the woman leaves Dunia's side. After she moves from her view, Dunia lays there for a long time. She can hear the crackle of a fire and smell the woodsmoke. There's a clank and clatter of dishes and the sizzle of meat. Dunia's mouth fills with saliva and she feels her stomach growl. She realizes how hungry she is. Dunia breathes deeply and the smell of onion and spices fills her nostrils. She needs to move. She needs to eat. She is pulled back to life by every human need she has, all at once. Dunia rolls over. She can see the mother bent over the fire, turning over pieces of meat and then stirring the contents of a blackened pot. Dunia presses her arms into the straw mat she's been laying on, and sits up slowly. Her body feels stiff from lying in the same position for a long time. Dunia massages her neck and turns her head from side to side and there he is. The man with the amber eyes is looking at her.

"You!" she croaks. She pauses, surprised by the sound of her own voice.

The man gets up and brings her a gourd of water. Dunia drinks. She nods her head, wipes her mouth and points at the man, "I knew you had fresh water."

The man doesn't register any understanding, but Dunia laughs anyway. She's amazed that her circuitous path has led her right here into the home of this man. She finds it funny that her steady obsession with water, cut short by her long sleep, is right here waiting for her upon waking.

The man continues to look at her, not understanding her expression.

"I'm alive," she says, "I'm going to live."

At that moment, the mother enters the hut in a bustle, calling out to her children. The children run in one after the other and sit cross legged at a small round table. The girl sticks out her tongue and makes a face at her brother. The mother lays out food – cooked meat, stewed vegetables and a bowl filled with berries of some kind. Dunia can't take her eyes off the food. The mother speaks again to her children and the girl gets up and leads Dunia to the table. Then she shows her how to sit and passes her a wooden bowl. The man with the amber eyes – the father joins them. He bows his head and the family follows his example as the man speaks a blessing. That voice. She knows that voice. It was him, praying and speaking those words of blessing. Dunia's eyes fill with tears. They drip down her cheeks and spill down her neck onto her chest. This beautiful family saved her life. And they are held together by God, the same way her own family is. When the boy looks up from his prayer and sees Dunia's face, he gets up and gently wipes her tears onto his grubby sleeve. The mother tries to stop him, holding out a clean piece of fabric toward Dunia. Dunia and the mother exchange a look and a moment of tension before breaking into peals of laughter. The boy looks from one face to the next, with no idea what's so funny.

36

ALLAH

Dunia lies back on her straw mat, head propped up on her arms and watches Asim as he performs his afternoon prayers. Asim is the man with the amber eyes. She's learned the names of all the family members and some of the neighbors that know she's here, hidden away in the corner of the hut on an overstuffed straw mat. The hut is her whole world. She can't go outside during the day because she risks being seen by soldiers or officers patrolling the island. She has to stay hidden away to protect the family and the village. She takes that very seriously. Niazmina and Rakeem have become like a niece and nephew to her. They make her think of her own children. Their antics and play are no different than the things she witnessed back home as part of everyday life.

Right on cue with her thoughts, Rakeem bursts into the hut and announces something loudly before slapping his hand across his mouth, realizing that his father is at prayer. He looks at Dunia, eyes big and tiptoes backwards out of the hut with his hand held fast across his mouth. In his other hand he is carrying a long jagged stick. He is often bursting in and announcing things loudly. And often running around with a stick! Dunia loves him for it. She lies back again on her straw mat and smiles to herself. She is biding her time. Sometimes, Saleema, the mother, asks her to help out with the cleaning or the cooking inside the hut. Dunia loves to see and smell the spices and herbs Saleema has grown in her garden or foraged from the woods - ingredients and flavors Dunia has never experienced before.

She thinks, 'If I ever get back home, my cooking will never be the same.'

Most of Dunia's day is spent hiding out, laying and resting on her straw mat. She's never done so little for so long in her whole life, and it's harder than it looks. To be still, with all of her thoughts and without knowing her future, the fate of her family, the state of things back on the mainland, when or if she will ever be able to return to her home. There are so many unknowns and she's become intimate with the feelings that go along with all of them. She spends several hours every day steeping in it. There's nowhere to run and there's nowhere to hide. And it hurts. Sometimes she weeps desperately. Or lays back as hot tears stream down her cheeks and into her hair, partially gray now and spread out all around her on the mat. She's haunted by thoughts of Mary, her youngest child, the one she couldn't protect. She thinks about Jacob and her intuition that he has left this world. And that her children have all been left to fend for themselves.

'How have they fared?' she asks herself, 'Who has survived? And are they facing themselves as I am facing myself?'

Asim raises his hands in the air and calls out to Allah. Dunia watches him bend at the waist, hands held in prayer position. Allah is his God. Dunia has figured this out by watching him pray five times a day. She's learned his words and intonations and could repeat every sound to perfection without fully understanding its meaning. Although ultimately, she feels that she does understand its meaning. This man is as dedicated to his God as she is to hers.

'I wonder if we pray to the same God?' Dunia thinks, 'Same God, different name.'

Asim's prayer breaks up the monotony of the day. It interrupts Dunia's unending train of thought and brings her back to God.

"Allah," she whispers the word out loud.

Asim is on his knees, bending forward and bringing his forehead down toward the ground to rest for a moment on his red and gold fringed prayer mat. Dunia is still mystified by the bright colors the family has in their clothing and textiles. She wonders if their knowledge could help improve her family's trade. It's a funny thought as she has no idea what she has to go back to in Kobeliaky. But part of her still pictures Maroushka there, in the family hut, stirring flowers into a big pot and creating purple elderberry dye.

That night during supper, Saleema shares that a boat has been spotted near the dock. There are rumors that they are picking up prisoners and taking them off of the island. This exchange occurs between Dunia and Saleema, with each using their best knowledge of each other's language and Rakeem jumping in to act out Saleema's sentences, to help

Dunia understand. With a lot of back and forth between the two and jumping up and down by Rakeem, Dunia finally understands. Rakeem sits back and rests, chest heaving as if he's run a race.

"Is the war over?" Dunia asks, brow furrowed.

Of course Saleema and Asim have no way to answer this even if they did speak the same language.

Dunia knows that she needs to leave the village. Tomorrow she must go and make her way to the place where she was dropped off by the ship. If another ship comes, she needs to be there to board it and find her way back home.

Asim watches Dunia's face as the information registers. He knows she can't stay here forever and that she needs to find her way back to her village and to her family. He knows that she has people waiting for her, looking for her. Even still, his heart aches at the thought of her leaving. He never wanted her here in the first place. He fought hard to keep her away. But Allah had other plans. And now it feels hard to say goodbye. Asim keeps his thoughts and feelings to himself, allowing the children one final meal with Dunia before they understand what has to happen next.

Niazmina holds out the bowl of bread for Rakeem but holds it a few inches short of his grasp. Every time he reaches a little further for it, she pulls it back ever so slightly, goading him. Rakeem pounds his fist on the table and announces something loudly and Niazmina hands over the bowl with an innocent look on her face. The game is not lost on anyone.

'How will I possibly say goodbye?' Dunia thinks.

Knowing this is her last meal with the family, Dunia suddenly wants time to slow down. She has spent so many hours lamenting the time, finding it so difficult to lie still and be, and now, all at once, she feels the need to savor every last moment. She wants to capture every exchange and every flavor. Once she leaves the island of Prorva, she knows she will never return. And her time here will fade as every memory does. She longs to etch it into her heart and mind. To remember the feeling of belonging she found in such a strange and foreign place.

'Families are the same everywhere,' she thinks, 'We are all made of the same stuff.'

Dunia looks around the table. She sees the light in everyone's eyes. Asim makes eye contact just for a moment and Dunia can see his eyes are wet. She knows that in his wisdom, he understands this too.

37

GOODBYE

That night, Dunia decides to stay for one more day to say goodbye and to give the children a chance to get used to the idea that she is leaving.

Rakeem acts out what he wants to say which is essentially 'Why do you have to leave?' He's been crying all morning since Saleema broke the news to them. Niazmina isn't talking to Dunia right now. She's off licking her wounds somewhere and Dunia understands. She only hopes Niazmina will come to a place of acceptance so they can say a proper goodbye.

Dunia will leave in the early hours of the morning under the cover of darkness. Asim has agreed to accompany her beyond the boundaries of the village. He wants to see her safely across the island and make sure that no one spots her. Of course, he could never be sure of that, but it feels right that he should go with her part of the way. Perhaps to the place he encountered her in the woods several months ago. He's sure that she knows her way back from there. It will also give Saleema a chance to tend to the children and their sadness around Dunia's farewell.

Rakeem reaches out for Dunia and buries his face in her dress. She lifts him up and cradles him in her arms.

"U tebe ye khlopets[1]?" he asks in broken Ukrainian. In the short time Dunia has been there, Niazmina and Rakeem have picked up her language at a pace reserved only for the curious and malleable minds of children.

"I have three," she says, holding up three fingers and smiling down at him.

"Three?" he says in surprise. Rakeem mulls it over while twisting a strand of Dunia's hair between his fingers.

"They must miss you," he says, letting go of his grip on Dunia's arm.

She holds him there for a long time. The sun is starting to stream in through the doors of the hut and with it, the shouts and laughter of the village children. Finally, Rakeem's curiosity gets the better of him and he climbs out of Dunia's arms and runs out the door, into the sunlight.

'He'll be okay,' Dunia thinks watching him leave. She sits there for a few minutes listening to his voice in chorus with his friends. "He is so loud," Dunia says, chuckling.

Dunia helps Saleema with supper and late in the afternoon, Niazmina enters the hut, watching quietly as Dunia and her mother work.

---

1. Do you have a boy?

"Can I help?" she asks her mother.

Saleema moves aside and lets Niazmina into the space between her and Dunia.

Dunia can feel the warmth of Niazmina as she works next to her. After a long time in silence, Niazmina looks up at Dunia.

"I'll miss you," she says. Saleema looks at Dunia to try and understand what's been said. Dunia gives the girl a hug, careful not to get the onion and spices from her hands onto Niazmina's dress. The three of them continue to work together quietly preparing their final meal together.

That night, Dunia helps Saleema tuck the children into bed. She admires their sleepy faces looking up at her. Rakeem is clutching something in his hand and when his mother asks about it, he reveals a rock with white crystals in it. Saleema admires it before putting it up on the shelf for safe keeping. She kisses her son on the forehead and tucks the covers in all around him. Then she tucks in Niazmina and begins to sing a lullaby. The tune is like nothing Dunia has ever heard before. It starts out soft and sweet and moves into something more heartbreaking at the chorus. The feeling fits the moment. Afterwards, Niazmina asks Dunia if she can sing one too. Dunia thinks for a minute. Then she sings the song about the little mosquito on his wedding day. It's tragic too but only for a mosquito, so it doesn't feel so bad.

As Dunia lies down to sleep, she can hear Niazmina humming the tune. Then she drifts off to sleep.

Asim wakes Dunia in the early hours of the morning.

"It's time to go," he whispers.

Dunia understands and gathers her belongings. They are already packed together with some food and water. She leaves with her original bottles now filled to the brim with fresh spring water from the village.

At the entrance of the cottage, Dunia embraces Saleema and kisses her on the cheek. The children are gathered by the door, sleepy-eyed and tousle-haired. Dunia embraces each of them.

"Goodbye my dear ones," she says.

"Goodbye," Rakeem says, rubbing his eyes.

"Goodbye," Niazmina says, handing her a green scarf. It's the one she was wearing around her head the day Dunia first saw her.

Dunia is touched by the gift but looks at Saleema, to make sure it's okay.

Saleema smiles and nods, tears in her eyes.

Dunia admires the color, amazed at its richness. It reminds her of Zelenyy Lis[2] near her home growing up in Kobeliaky. She aches for home.

And just like that, Dunia steps out into the night with Asim close behind. The sky is clear with a crescent moon and stars twinkling above. The air is cool and a mist hangs low in the field beyond the village. Dunia wants to wear the scarf but instead tucks it deep into her bag. She wants no visible evidence of where she's been hiding for the last few months.

---

2. The Green Forest

Dunia and Asim follow the path leading out of the village and into the woods. They move quietly, looking from left to right, making sure that all is quiet. The path leads around and upwards to a hill that overlooks the village. Dunia stands on the crest of the hill catching her breath and looks back. This was the place that she first saw the Native village. It looks different to her now. People that she loves live there. The morning is still and the sky is only beginning to lighten.

"This way," Asim calls out.

They continue down the path and into the darkness of the woods. Dunia can hear the sound of their footsteps. Asim is ahead now and Dunia steps where he steps following him closely. The woods are quiet, other than the sound of her breath.

Even the birds are still sleeping up in the trees, heads tucked gently under their wings.

The path runs parallel to the beach and Dunia hears the rush of the surf before she sees the rocky shoreline. It begins as a white noise that gives way to soft rhythmic lapping. Dunia loves the sound. She knows exactly where she is now and she can make out the shapes of the rocks on the shoreline. This is the spot where she hid behind the rocks from the family of natives.

When she looks ahead, Asim is facing her.

"You know the way," he says.

It's not a question, but Dunia nods at him, assuring him that she will be okay from here. She reaches out her hand and touches his arm. He bows slightly. The sky is brighter now and when he looks down at her, she sees the beautiful color of his eyes. And then he is gone, back down the path toward his home. Dunia watches him go and then turns in the direction of her home -toward the old dock, hanging onto the prayer of an unknown ship coming to take her home.

38

THE SHIP

A ship is resting next to the dock as Dunia approaches the rocky shoreline. She had envisioned herself camping out in the woods for several days before the arrival of a ship, rationing her water and living off the land. But instead, the boat is waiting for her at port, as if she purchased her ticket for a pleasure cruise and arrived in perfect time for the next departure. From a distance, the ship looks like a child's toy bobbing gently up and down in the surf. But as Dunia approaches, she is dwarfed by its size. The vessel has been moored there for several days and continues to do so for several more days after Dunia's arrival.

As she crosses the beach toward the dock, she can see that the bloody rocks have been washed clean by the waves and there is no trace of the carnage of her arrival. Just barnacles and seaweed strewn among the rocks and a few orange and purple sea stars clinging to the stones near the shoreline. The sea has washed everything clean. She walks the length of the dock and boards the ship casually and without event. There are no words from the officers patrolling the deck. She doesn't wait or ask permission, she simply walks aboard and takes a seat on a wooden bench.

Again, she has the strange feeling that she is a paid passenger headed home after a trip to visit family. There is no mention that she's been left for dead on "an island with no fresh water," and no question about how she survived it. She did, and that seems to pay the toll for her passage back to the mainland. It's as if the insanity of her arrival and of her entire time served here has blown over and these men have moved on to other things. The whole thing swept neatly under the rug.

In fact, Dunia doesn't recognize any of the deckhands or officers from her trip over and there's no one to point her anger at. These are an entirely new crew and their sins are yet unknown to her. They are all busy moving this way and that, preparing the ship for the next leg of its voyage. One man, struggling to carry a large piece of pipe, moves past her, to a metal stairway leading down into the bowels of the ship. He grunts and groans as he passes. Another man whistles tunelessly, as he mops an upper section of the deck. Several officers are standing in the sun in the bow of the ship, smoking cigarettes and chatting quietly.

Dunia rests and waits. She sees that other prisoners have made their way onto the ship and are gathering their tattered edges together, in various corners. Some appear to have done okay, while others appear more like frightened animals.

One woman sits near the stern of the ship. She is unkempt, clutching her meager belongings to her chest, rocking back and forth, a vacant look in her eyes. Every once in a while she shouts out something in a language Dunia doesn't understand. When Dunia hears the commotion, she looks at the woman, startled by the intensity of her cries, straining to understand the dialect. But as time goes on and the yelling continues, she doesn't bother. She realizes the woman isn't communicating anything in particular, just bawling like a wounded animal. Dunia hopes the ship's crew will give the woman a wide berth. Dunia has no idea what the rules or limitations are on this boat and she intends to stay out of the way and not draw attention to herself.

As the day wears on, more prisoners make their way out of the woods and the wild of the island and down the slanted wooden dock onto the ship. They appear in varying states of disarray. One man boards and sits down on the floor of the ship near Dunia. His hair and beard are thick, shaggy and matted with dirt. Dunia can smell him even though the breeze is blowing in her favor. He smells like a bear…or maybe worse, but when he senses Dunia looking at him he makes eye contact and smiles through his fur.

That's a very civilized smile, Dunia thinks, *Aside from a desperate need for a bath, he looks like he fared well.*

The man's cheeks are rosy and he seems to carry a certain pride at having survived the island. He has several dead animals on his belt. They look like rabbits, or squirrels. Dunia understands his pride. It feels like a big "Fuck you!" to the bastards that left them here to die.

I wonder if he had help? Dunia ponders.

"Do you speak Ukrainian?" Dunia asks.

"Yes, hello sister" the man replies.

Dunia moves toward him, overcome with excitement to connect with her countryman but she stops mid-step, held back by the wall of his stench.

"I know," he says, with a laugh, "I smell like a beast!"

Dunia laughs, relieved at him stating the obvious and moves back to the bench to continue their conversation at a distance.

The two of them cannot speak fast enough. Dunia is overwhelmed by the power of speaking in her mother tongue and being understood. She pauses for a moment, mid-sentence, and looks around to see if the officers or deckhands are listening. She has learned to guard her words. But nobody is paying attention to them. The crew men are engrossed in their tasks and probably don't speak her language anyway. Dunia turns back to the man.

"Who are you?" she asks.

"I'm Boryslav,"

They begin exchanging stories and information with an urgency that comes from both being cut off from human connection by language barriers and surviving an impossible situation designed to kill them.

Dunia learns that there was a small underground stream toward the other side of the island from the village and Boryslav survived by trapping animals and foraging from the forest.

"The sea water is thick with fish too. I could reach in and grab supper with my hands," he says holding out two massive paws in front of him.

As the conversation rolls on, Dunia learns that he grew up only a few miles away from her home in Kobeliaky.

"I bet you look very civilized underneath all the hair," Dunia says with a smile.

"Yes!" he says laughing, "I was a school teacher."

Dunia is so surprised by the news that she sits back on the bench for a moment to take it in.

"So was my father," she says, leaning forward towards the man once again.

Dunia thinks to herself, *You can never tell what people are made of by looking at them. Why does it continue to surprise me?*

"I taught math and music," Boryslav adds.

The conversation comes to a lull here, as Boryslav looks out over the water, lost in thought. Dunia is thinking about her father and all the lessons he taught her. She is transported back to Kobeliaky on a sunny afternoon in the garden of their hut. In her mind she is home and Nepefan is seated on a wooden stump explaining the meaning of a poem about a copper colored river. He explains that the poem is about love and its unending flow.

After a time, Dunia is drawn back to the moment by a cool breeze that rushes in off the water. She breaks the silence, "Well we must connect again for a civilized meal at my home in Kobeliaky."

"I'll ride my horse there," he says, as if he's sure the mare is still there, grazing in the woods near his home, where he left her.

They both smile at the possibility but a sad question lingers in both of their minds.

Will we be released when we reach the mainland, or will we continue our prison sentence in a different cell?

39

1938: THE GREAT PURGE

A letter from a Polish man trapped in the Soviet Union, to his wife in Romania. Many letters like this were intercepted by the communist government and never delivered to their rightful owners. The government used this "intelligence" to track down their opponents. So many efforts at communication were stolen and so many words left unspoken between friends, lovers and family members.

Dear Nataliya,

My beautiful wife, I miss you. Please forgive me for staying.

I'm so glad that you and Nina left for Romania when you did. I needed you to be somewhere safe. I needed to protect you... don't begrudge me that. A husband must protect his wife and children. It is my duty. I picture you there with the cows and the forest and the fields aflame with pink rhododendrons and I feel that I have done something right in my life.

I can still see the expression on your face as the train pulled out of the station - first shock and then absolute fury. I thought a lot about what you might have said to me at that moment, if the train hadn't pulled away with a lurch. No matter how it changes, it always starts with "You bastard!"

I'm sorry that I had to stay behind. I'm sorry for deceiving you. I just thought that there was something I could do here. And I thought it was the best way. Now, I'm not so sure. I'm not sure if that was the right thing to do and I'm not sure if there is anything I can do to help the situation here. But I do know that you never would have left me, given the choice.

Oh Nataliya, the world has tipped over on its axis. What's up is down and what's down is up. The story has been twisted into something I can't recognize anymore. I'm not sure that I have the strength to untangle it.

It's raining here today. The sky is dead and gray and honestly, I know how that feels. Today, I feel devoid of hope... except for you my love. You and Nina are everything in the world. And I imagine that the sun is shining where you are. I can see it shining on your beautiful face. I miss the smell of your hair and the glorious sway of your hips.

How is Nina doing? Does she miss her Papa? Is she still scared of the train? Tell her I'm safe and I'll join you just as soon as I can. Tell her I just had a few things to finish up here before coming to the farm. Tell her that I can't wait to bounce her on my knee again. And tell her to eat a plum for me.

I can still remember the first time she tasted a plum. We could barely pry it out of her hand to retrieve the stone. That was our last summer together before everything changed. We were so happy together -our little family and our time on the riverside. It feels like so long ago now. Drink some plum brandy for me, Nataliya. And say a prayer when you do. I need to find a pathway out of here and I can't see it right now. I'm afraid I could die here. I've wanted to shield you from all of this but I tried that and now I am full of regret.

I think about you all the time. You feel like the softest and sanest thing in the world to me. God I wish I had gotten on that train with you. I thought I could fight this. But it's absolute madness here. I don't know what's coming next. I know that you saw this coming. Never doubt your dreams. They've been warning you for a long time – giving you information. It's a realm that I don't understand. I doubted you. I'm sorry my love. I couldn't see beyond what my eyes were seeing. You are as much of an artist as I am. You're a visionary. I needed to feel like the leader. I'm sorry about so much.

I wanted to write something gentle and reassuring but you deserve to know the truth. It's a very dangerous time to be alive in the Soviet Union. It's dangerous to have a voice or a viewpoint that opposes the government. Artists, writers, intellectuals, we're the target. Any form of free expression, if you're caught, will lead to charges. The charges might be completely unrelated and even fabricated.

They planted evidence in Symon's apartment. That's what he kept shouting about when they came in the night and took him away on false charges. He was shouting about papers that had been hidden away, planted in his apartment. He kept saying it over and over as they dragged him down the hallway. Six men with guns and billy clubs come to take one man away. I just stood there helplessly with my hand up my ass. God, why didn't I fight them?! I couldn't even protect my friend. I haven't seen him since then. That was over a week ago now. I'm sure he faces incarceration or deportation. He might be dead, Nataliya. People are being tortured into confessions and then sent to the gulag to die. Or sometimes, if that's not fast enough the NKVD[1] *will murder them directly. I have heard the explosion of the firing squad at night. And I've gotten used to the sight of dead bodies on the road. It's like business as usual. We are expected to get up and go about our day acting as if all of this is normal.*

Stalin intends to crush anyone that opposes him or threatens his line of reasoning. Of course there is no reason here at all. There's only the insatiable hunger of a madman and his government of thugs. Symon explained it clearly in an article he wrote for the underground paper. He said it's as if there's an electric fence that's been built around their version of the "truth." And that anyone who dares to oppose it will receive a zap. Maybe that zap will be meant only to scare you into submission or slander your name. Or maybe it'll be intended to kill you. Or maybe that zap will be aimed at your loved ones while you look on helplessly, pleading to redact your previous opinion in order to save the lives of your wife, or your children. The point is, to speak your truth, out loud, in print or through any art form is to put your life in danger. This is why I'm so glad you're far away from this place. I only wish I was there with you.

It is possible that I won't be able to get out of here, Nataliya. I feel so lost and I just can't see the way out right now. I know that you would be able to see it if you were here. Don't ever stop speaking about what is happening here. And don't ever stop sharing your truth. Trust your gut. It has never led you wrong. The world needs to know that our country is in the clutches of a lunatic.

1. The People's Commissariat for Internal Affairs

I love you and I'll never give up. Please stay put if you can. It'll make it easier for me to find you. If you must go, then leave me a trail of "breadcrumbs" like we talked about. You are the love of my life- my queen, my empress.

Give my love to Nina

And take good care of yourself.

Yours,
Vitaliy

40

1939: THE PROFESSOR

Dunia will be put to work caring for a dying man. Another dying man! There is no shortage of them, it seems. Dunia has seen so much death that it doesn't surprise her or upset her anymore. She has seen bodies rotting at the side of the road, their lips pulled back in a vacuous grimace. She has seen men killed right before her eyes, their blood spilled over the rocky shoreline. She witnessed a look of absolute peace descend on the face of a boy as he finally submitted to starvation and exposure on a cold and cobbled street in Dnepropetrovsk. And then, on the Island of Prorva, she faced her own death. It doesn't scare her anymore. Death has been a constant companion on her journey and yet, it hasn't come to claim her.

"I must have more work to do," she says to her cell mates the day before she leaves the prison, "If God had wanted me dead, He would have taken me already." One woman nods, taking in her words and wringing the fabric of her skirt with her hands. The others aren't really listening. They are lost in varying degrees of hunger and fear around the uncertainty of their circumstances.

Dunia is only there for three days. Where? She doesn't know. Some prison, somewhere. She couldn't point it out on a map. She's holed up in a dank cell with a handful of women and an armful of rats that come and go through the prison bars as if this is *their* home and the prisoners are the unwelcome guests. Dunia is there for three days and three nights before fate turns its hand.

The soldiers are speaking in Russian.

She can't understand everything she hears but she can make out the general flow of conversation. They're deciding what to do with the latest lot of prisoners. Those are their words and Dunia hears one soldier refer to them as, "This broken lot."

She hears talk of a gulag and of a train heading north. And she hears mention of another prison. One officer makes a joke about rape.

"We'll fuck them to death and then they'll be off our hands."

But no one laughs. No one is in the mood for his antics. Not after what happened last night. Last night, a woman in Dunia's cell went berserk. She screamed and raged at the guards saying, "You'll atone for your sins! God has seen what you've done and your day will come soon!" At first the men laughed, saying that the woman had gone mad. But she went on and on, preaching into the night and slamming her hands against the bars shouting "He's coming for you, He sees everything!" At some point, her words started to hit a nerve. Eventually the men couldn't stand it anymore. They ripped her from the cell and took her away. Dunia hasn't seen her since. But her message still hangs in the air.

The soldiers called her mad, trying to brush off what they heard. But Dunia knows the woman was perfectly sane. And she holds her own rage together with care. She has pressed her nails into the palm of her own hand and drawn blood in an effort to hold back the flurry of slaps and punches she has wanted to throw, she has bit down on her own tongue not to say the words she has wanted to say, not to scream and yell and let the raw truth tumble out of her mouth in a fury. It has taken tremendous strength to hold back her natural response to the injustice she has experienced and witnessed. This restraint has kept her alive. But she understands how easy it would be to lose control and let the flood of everything she's been holding back pour forth onto these bastards. It is only the grace of God now that keeps her from doing it.

The soldiers shuffle around. Three men leave, including the "rape joke" soldier. Two soldiers remain. Dunia watches through the veil of her hair. She listens. One man lights a cigarette and blows smoke up toward a small open window in the concrete wall. They speak more softly now. The younger of the two men begins to share about a professor. The man is dying. Is it his father-in-law? His grandfather? The details are lost in their hushed tones, the rush of the wind blowing in the trees outside the window and the sound of a prisoner crying and wailing down the hall.

"He's dying of wasting disease," the man says, "he looks like a shadow." The man turns away and continues to talk.

Dunia loses the thread for a while. Finally, he turns back in her direction saying, "Someone needs to take care of him."

Dunia understands that this man owes the professor a favor. Was he raised by the man? Educated by him? The story comes out. Dunia recognizes that there is a connection back to the man's childhood. She sees a glimmer of the little boy inside the man. It emerges intermittently, as he speaks about the professor.

"I've done that before," Dunia says to the soldiers, recognizing her moment. The men turn toward her, surprised to see her face staring back at them through the prison bars.

"I took care of an official in the gulag five years ago," Dunia presses on.

"Who asked you!?" The young soldier snaps back.

"No, no," the older man says soothingly, holding out his hands toward his friend and calming the moment. He turns and says something to his friend. Something that Dunia can't hear. But she can sense that this man might back her solution.

Dunia waits a full minute, swallowing her fear, allowing the young man to relax.

"He fattened up and got healthier under my care," Dunia adds, "I've raised children and I can grow a garden too."

Dunia never could have anticipated that her skills as a mother would have spared her from the gulag, not once, but twice. Three times if you count the time she spent mothering prostitutes at the experimental farm.

The following morning, she is taken from her cell. When she steps outside, she takes a deep breath and notices how sweet the air is and how bright the colors are. The sun is streaming in sideways onto the concrete compound outside the prison doors. And to Dunia, it looks beautiful. She can see a low lying mist crawling its way across a grassy field in the distance. And a lone deer is feeding on grass and shrubs, head bent low. Nobody seems to see it but her. The sun is shining on its white speckled hide. It's a fawn.

"Where is its mother?" Dunia wonders.

From there she is put on a truck, a train and then another truck. She travels for a long time. She is taken far into the Russian countryside. As she travels along, the evidence of war dissipates and then disappears altogether. It is replaced by a beautiful natural landscape; soft rolling hills, a blue lake and a cluster of trees with bright green leaves shimmering in the breeze. Finally, she lands, exhausted, on the crumbling steps of the professor's cottage. It's mid-summer, and fresh green ivy has crawled its way up the side of the building and spread out to cover its surface. The sun shines down on the ivy and Dunia can see the light green veins and arteries within each leaf. She can hear a cow lowing somewhere nearby and recognizes it as an urgent call to be milked.

When Dunia enters the cottage, she can smell the old man. She sees the place is in disarray and needs to be scrubbed down too. She sees plates encrusted with the remains of meals, half-eaten. She sees soiled clothing strewn here and there. She sees newspapers open, spread out over the surface of every table and sections of the floor too. She sees a piss pot brimming and a curious dark stain on the carpet right next to it. The man himself is withered and old and Dunia can tell that he won't be here for much longer. She can tell by his appearance; the sallow skin, the protruding ribs and the dark bags under his eyes, but also by the way he speaks. He holds nothing back, referring to Stalin as "the Lunatic," regardless of who is in the room.

"I know what's right and what's wrong," he says, "and that's all there is to it." Everyone within earshot is going to hear about it and Dunia recognizes that he too, has nothing to lose. When the soldier presents her as his new nursemaid, the professor responds by blowing a raspberry through his lips and referring to the soldier's gun as his "Cock extension."

The Professor has escaped deportation, even though he's an academic. Books line the walls of the cottage and where the books can no longer fit on the shelves, they stand in great, tall stacks. The man has built himself a fortress of books and only on good days does he have the strength to hobble over to the shelf and retrieve one. Often, he'll read for only a minute or two before drifting off into slumber, his mouth agape. He seems to have some connection to the military, perhaps the reason he remains protected. He refers to Dunia as his "body guard," and she takes the task seriously, serving him peppermint tea to calm the contents of his curdled stomach.

He has an old gramophone. Dunia has never seen one before this. One afternoon he wants to hear a particular song. He says, "I've been hearing it in my dreams." So Dunia figures out how to use the device, with the help of his disjointed instructions. The man is laying in his bed with the sheets pulled up to his chin, trying his best to explain how the thing works. Finally, a beautiful melody pours out and fills the room. The professor sits up in bed. "Tchaikovsky," he says breathlessly, hand to his heart. Then he settles back down onto the pillows and dozes the rest of the afternoon, waking only when the music stops to say "Again, again."

41

THE RIVER

PLYVE KACHA PO TYSYNI

The Duck Floats Down The Tisina

Dunia walks by the river's edge. The water swirls and eddies below. It's a beautiful turquoise in the shallows and rich blue towards the middle, where the water gets deeper. There are grasses, reeds, rushes and sedges growing along the edge of the river and they drape into the water, flowing this way and that, like a woman's skirt. Cattails decorate the opposite shore, the sun illuminating their fuzzy brown heads. Dunia watches a family of muskrats swimming in and out of their den, moving like acrobats through the water. She wonders about all of the secret caverns of their underground world. What do they see under there? They are beautiful and graceful creatures in spite of their name. Dunia continues to walk. Cherry trees grow along the pathway. She stops to taste their fruit. Each one tastes a little different. It must be the variance in soil quality, the amount of sun and perhaps some other unknown and immeasurable factors. Maroushka would know more about it. Dunia wishes she could ask her. She spits a cherry pit into the grass, high as her waist, and looks out across the valley. The landscape is vibrant and the sun is warm on the back of her neck. She picks another handful of glossy rubies from the tree. So far, *this* is her favorite tree. She puts her hand against it and feels the roughness of its bark. It's warm from the sun. Then she looks out over the landscape again, scanning for movement. Her first day out, she startled a cinnamon bear. He was high up a tree feasting on cherries. When he saw Dunia, he seemed afraid and tried to get away, higher up into the branches.

"Crack! Snap snap snap snap!" The branch broke and the bear tumbled down through the tree, snapping branches all the way down. He fell in a mad jumble of fur on the grass. It happened so fast, Dunia had no time to react. She stood there, stunned, watching; waiting to see what he would do next. The bear bellowed, like a child, and ran off into the woods. Once he reached the edge of the woods, he stopped and looked back at her shyly. He seemed uninjured from the fall. He looked small for a bear and Dunia wondered if he was, in fact, a child. Dunia hasn't seen him since, but she's cautious. She pops another cherry into her mouth.

'How could he resist this place,' she thinks. She picks another handful of fruit and puts it into her apron pocket. She'll take it back for the professor. Try to entice him to eat something.

Every afternoon the professor takes a nap. At first Dunia refused to leave him, worried about his condition and what might happen in her absence.

"I promise not to die while you're away," he said firmly and with a slight upturn at the corner of his lips. The man wants his solitude. “I’ve spent most of my life alone and I like it that way,” he said, making his case.

Dunia looked at him doubtfully.

“I’m a grown man and I can be alone if I want to,” he stated, his hand in a fist.

Dunia smiled.

Then he softened and pleaded, “Give me a moment’s peace, I’m only waiting to die anyways.”

So Dunia agreed.

And every day, after lunch, she puts him to bed, tucks him in and sets a glass of water on the bedside table. “Don’t die while I’m awaaaaay,” she says in a sing-song way as she puts on her shoes.

“I woooon’t,” he sings back.

This is their little joke.

Then Dunia heads out the cottage door, past the cow that she has named Anastasia, and down the path, toward the river and toward her beloved cherry trees.

Anastasia greets her every morning with a “Maaaah!”

Dunia goes out to collect water from the well for the professor’s breakfast. She puts the water to boil on the fire for their porridge and then walks back across the yard to milk the cow, grabbing a metal bucket that has found its home on an old fence post. Anastasia is very affectionate and she nuzzles her gentle head towards Dunia. She is so happy that someone is taking care of her with consistency. Her milk is gloriously creamy and Dunia can't remember the last time she tasted anything like it. The professor drinks a small glass and the rest is left to Dunia. She's been drinking fresh milk every morning with her breakfast. So fresh, it's still warm. Then she has another glass in the evening, so nothing goes to waste. She can feel herself getting stronger.

"Your cheeks look rosy," the professor said this morning, as Dunia helped him into his cardigan, "I thought you came here to help *me* heal."

"Some people are beyond help!" Dunia retorts, gesturing toward him and wondering suddenly if she went too far. But the man laughs. He takes it as well as he dishes it out. Death isn't a serious topic for them. They both know it's coming.

Dunia has been taking afternoon walks for two weeks, since agreeing to leave the professor alone for his afternoon nap, and the cherries have gone from sweet to sweeter as the days have passed. Today, they are heavenly and Dunia wipes the crimson juice from her chin.

Then she finds a comfortable patch of grass and settles herself down to watch the river flowing. A family of ducks are bobbing around noiselessly upstream.

"Waaah, waah," one of them breaks the silence.

They take turns feeding underwater, bums pointed straight up in the air. Dunia thinks of Ivan, her eldest son. When he was little, the whole family would walk together, after church on Sunday, down to Galina's pond. They would bring a heel of bread to feed the ducks. But Ivan would always nibble away at it and often there was very little left for the birds. He loved bread! She can remember how he would help her bake in the kitchen, kneading his own dough and forming a little chicky out of it. Dunia would add two cloves for eyes and then bake it. He loved eating it with fresh butter. He was so interested in the way the bread rose; like magic to his five year old mind.

Suddenly, Dunia is overcome by emotion. Where is her son? Where are her babies? She watches the water flow past her and tears stream down her cheeks. The ducks don't pay attention to her. She weeps and wails and they go on feeding, tail feathers pointed skyward. The river continues to flow and the sun continues to shine. Time passes. And after a while, she's calm again. The flow of the river has her in a trance. And she has a vision of Ivan. He's alive. She feels a connection with him. She can see him building something, working with his hands. His skin is brown, like his Dad's would get during the summer. She can see the wiry muscles of his arms. He's lean but strong and very much alive. The place where he works reminds her of the streets of Dnepropetrovsk.

42

ANOTHER PLACE

AUGUST

The cherries are past their prime and creeping bellflowers have opened up along the side of the path. They sway in the breeze. Grasshoppers jump left and right as Dunia meanders back toward the cottage. The heat of late afternoon shimmers ahead of her, hovering above the grass like a wave. Earlier today she wandered out towards the wood in search of some shade. She searched the forest floor for mushrooms. The professor has been eating less and less over the past month, and yesterday he refused his supper. Part of her thinks the right ingredients might tempt him back toward life. But another part of her knows that refusing food happens naturally toward the end of life. She's not ready to say goodbye yet. 'I've said too many goodbyes,' she thinks to herself. But another thought troubles her too, "where will my path lead once my work here is done?" Dunia shivers in spite of the heat. She didn't find what she was looking for in the woods but instead, returns with her apron pocket filled with wild garlic. *I smell like Ukrainian sausage,* she says to herself.

She walks past Anastasia who is resting in the shade of an oak tree. The cow looks at Dunia and twitches her ears lazily, chasing off a fly. Dunia feels like she's moving through molasses and her legs ache as she walks the stone path towards the cottage. The heat causes everything to move more slowly. Dunia steps into the cottage and looks toward the bed where the professor lies. Her eyes take a minute to adjust to the darkness of the room. It's a few degrees cooler in here, thanks to the earthen walls. The professor lays quietly in his bed. Dunia touches him. His skin is still warm. But he looks smaller -even smaller than he did yesterday.

"I brought wild garlic for our supper," Dunia says brightly.

"Hmmmm," the professor responds, opening his eyes.

"I'm going outside to cook," she says, "Do you need anything?"

The professor shakes his head and closes his eyes again.

Dunia makes a salad out of potatoes, wild garlic and cream. She boils a few eggs and cuts two large wedges of cheese for their supper. She presents it to the professor. "You must eat," she says.

But the professor turns his head away from her.

Dunia puts the meal on a side table and offers him a glass of milk. He accepts a few sips and then requests water. Dunia sits on the grass in the yard in the shade of the cottage and finishes her meal alone. She looks out across the meadow. There is a heaviness that has wrapped itself around her heart. It reminds her of the day the women were separated at the experimental farm. She can still see

Tatiana's stunned expression, staring out at her through the front window of the farm house, as the truck lurched away, down the lane.

'It nearly over,' she finally says to herself.

The next morning Dunia wakes up and checks on the professor. He's breathing slowly and lying very still. Dunia goes outside and takes care of Anastasia who is waiting patiently by the fence. Dunia puts her hand against the cow's flank. Then she rests her head against the creature's side and takes in her warmth. Finally, Dunia puts her arms around the cow's neck and gives her a loving squeeze.

"Thank you," Dunia says, suddenly grateful for the cow; her warmth, her nourishment and her humble presence.

"Maaaah," Anastasia responds.

Dunia makes breakfast for one. She offers the professor milk. She sits him up in bed and helps him to drink. It takes a long time. He drinks a small glass and then lays down again, exhausted. He says nothing.

Dunia tends to the chores. She cleans up the cottage and sorts out the yard. There are vegetables growing here. They've been planted willy-nilly, maybe by the professor, or a past housekeeper. There are several chickens around too. The birds had taken to the woods when Dunia first arrived but have made their way back sensing that someone reliable is tending the space. Fresh grain scattered around here and there helped to lure them home.

That afternoon she can't bring herself to leave the professor for her walk. So instead she runs her finger down the spines of a large stack of books, looking for something that she can read to him.

"The Kingdom of God is Within You," she reads, "By Leo Tolstoy."

And this is how the afternoon passes.

Dunia is seated on a faded blue cushion on the wooden chair reading aloud. And the professor is laying in bed, quite still. Dunia can smell the grass and the river and something sweet blowing in on the breeze through the window and out of the door which is propped open with an old leather boot. The sound of birds twittering and tumbling around in the lilac bushes in the yard can be heard through the open door. Their songs are punctuated by the occasional "Maaaah," as Anastasia searches the yard for a fresh patch of grass, alfalfa and clover.

Dunia reads, "The most difficult subjects can be explained to the most slow-witted man if he has not formed any idea of them already; but the simplest thing cannot be made clear to the most intelligent man if he is firmly persuaded that he knows already, without a shadow of doubt, what is laid before him."

After a time, Dunia's eyes grow tired reading in the dim light and she sits silently, watching the professor doze and feeling quite tired herself. Occasionally, she gets up to check on him, take a closer look and make sure he's still breathing. It seems like he is somewhere else. It seems like all the problems of this world are no longer his to contemplate. He's going somewhere else and something, maybe God, or maybe his soul is preparing him to do that.

Later in the afternoon, the cottage grows dark and Dunia peers out the door to see enormous gray clouds gathering. She looks up to see a thin layer of white cloud moving swiftly across the sky. And to the west a thick and ominous, green cloud emerges. Dunia shivers. She can smell the rain on the wind before she sees the droplets land. Anastasia has already taken cover in the small wooden shed at the other end of the yard.

Dunia closes the window so the rain drops don't land on a leaning stack of the professor's books. But she keeps the door open a crack, so they can listen to the rain and smell the fresh clean air. It comes into the space in great gusts, as if the cottage itself is taking a giant, sweet breath. Dunia wraps a shawl around her shoulders and settles herself back on the chair.

Then she sings.

She sings a song that she and Olena, her childhood friend, used to sing together. It's the one about the Little Bunny Boy. She can't remember all of the verses, so she makes up the words here and there and repeats what she knows. It takes her back to Kobeliaky- to a time when life felt so simple.

Then she remembers a song that she made up when she was little, and she sings that. She thinks about the way her father encouraged her to sing in the church choir. She decides not to sing church songs.

'It wouldn't be right,' she thinks, "The professor is not religious and this is his deathbed." She decides to honor *him* with her songs.

A beautiful lullaby comes to her next. It's the lullaby that Saleema sang to Niazmina and Rakeem on the island of Prorva. She doesn't know the words but she simply sings the sounds as she heard them. She sings the language of her friends without understanding its meaning. She knows enough to know that the words are filled with loving intention. The melody is laced with longing, she gets lost in it and when she looks toward the professor, she can see that his eyes are open. He's looking at her and his eyes have a shine to them. He's listening. He's present. Dunia takes hold of his hand and continues to sing, looking into his eyes. Her emotion weaves its way into the song, causing her voice to waver and break. Still, she sings on, looking back at his eyes and at his old weathered face. 'I'm seeing God. He is right here,' she thinks, as her heart brims and breaks.

After a while, her voice grows tired and they come into silence. The professor has closed his eyes. It's still raining outside; a gentle drumming against the roof and the splash of water on the leaves of the curly ivy plant, growing along the outside walls of the cottage. Dunia peers out the door. Everything has been washed clean and the green is more vibrant than ever.

"I'm going to make some supper," she says, turning back toward the professor.

All is quiet. She steps toward him and sees that he's gone.

Dunia breathes in quickly and then exhales, hand to her heart.

She sits down on her chair. She won't eat supper tonight. She'll sit here with him for a while and say goodbye.

43

BURYING THE PAST

The rain falls throughout the night and a clap of thunder draws Dunia out of a dream. Flashes of lightning illuminate the cottage, as a storm moves in from the west. Dunia sees the professor's body laid out on his bed where she left him. She lays awake, listening. The deluge contrasts the absolute stillness within the cottage. She is alone once again, absorbing her loss. She covered the professor with a sheet and turned his bed so his feet are facing toward the door. This is an old folk tradition and she doesn't know if he would have wished it or not. But it's something Maroushka taught her and so, it feels right. Traditionally the head of the body is turned toward a religious icon but the professor has none, so Dunia turned his head towards his books, which is not hard to do because they are everywhere. He loved books and they served as nourishment for his mind and soul.

The door and window remain open. 'That way the soul has a means of escape,' she can hear Maroushka's words in her mind. Dunia doesn't necessarily believe the folklore but it offers comfort. Death is sacred and it calls for the reverence of ritual. Tomorrow she will wash and prepare the body for burial. She has lost so many loved ones over the past six years.

'This is my chance to offer them all a proper burial,' she thinks.

Dunia wakes up late the next morning. The sun is streaming in through the cracks and a chicken has found its way into the cottage through the open door. She is clucking and bobbing her head up and down, scouring the floor for bugs.

"Shoo!" Dunia says from her sleeping mat.

The chicken looks at Dunia, undeterred. She cocks her head to the side, lets out another cluck and resumes her investigation.

Dunia is up on her feet, "Shoo, shoo!" she says, ushering the bird out the door. Dunia grabs a handful of grain from a bag in the cupboard and tosses it out into the yard. The chickens, which were scattered here and there, crowd in, pecking furiously. Anastasia hears the door creak open.

"Maahh!" she says, letting Dunia know what she needs. Life goes on.

After breakfast, Dunia washes and prepares the professor's body. She brushes his hair with pomade she finds in a small green jar on the bedside table. She feels a wave of sadness as she examines the items on the table; an empty glass of milk, a program from a performance of Lesia Ukrainka's "Forest song" at the National Academic Drama Theater in Kyiv, a silver comb, a folded blue handkerchief, a small brown bottle of cologne, a silver locket with a photo of a woman inside and the squat green jar of pomade. Dunia imagines the professor getting ready to go out, as a young man, looking like a gentleman and smelling like mint and something else she can't name. She holds the jar to her nose, trying to identify the smell. Next she soaps up the professor's chin and shaves off the patchy, gray stubble. "Cedar! It smells like cedar," she says out loud, thinking suddenly of Maroushka. Dunia remembers cuddling up with Baba when she was a little girl. She remembers how she and Maroushka would sit together on the grass as the sheep grazed in the field near Zelenyy Lis[1]. Dunia wipes the suds off of the professor's face with a warm cloth. She will leave him here to rest for two nights as the folk tradition suggests.

'This tradition may be a practical one,' Dunia thinks, "It allows me time to dig a grave."

There is an old shovel out in the shed and she plans to dig under the old oak tree, out past the yard and toward the river. It's a monumental task, but she has two days to do it and the downpour has softened up the earth in her favor.

"If I died here, I would want to be buried in the shade of that old tree," she says out loud.

"You'll be peaceful out there," she continues, talking to the professor, as if he is still with her. "And I'll plant tulips on your grave."

Dunia finds a fresh sheet and wraps the professor up in it.

1. The Green Forest

She puts a little dab of cologne behind each ear and on his wrist. Then she repositions the bed, which she turned in order to clean him properly.

"My husband died," she tells him, "Nobody told me that, I just know."

The afternoon is cool and the sky remains a steady gray. Dunia carries the shovel down to the old oak tree. She searches the ground for the right spot to begin her task. She sinks the tip of the shovel into the grass and digs. It isn't long before she has worked her way through the sod and made a small hole in the soft black earth. She is already sweating and wipes her forehead on the back of her sleeve. She removes her sweater and ties her hair up off of her shoulders. Anastasia has followed her over and is coming in for a curious look. Dunia digs for an hour before stopping to take a break. She wanders over to the well and drinks straight from the bucket letting the water drip down the front of her dress. She sits down on a mound of grass and stares off into the distance, catching her breath. She spends the rest of the afternoon working and resting, resting and working and by the time she has run out of steam, she has made significant progress. She leaves the shovel upright, stuck in a root bound mound of earth and makes her way back to the cottage to prepare a meal.

The next day she is up before the sun and works slowly but continuously, thinking about her family. She envisions Maroushka and her mother baking bread together, small loaves rising under a piece of cloth, in the warmth of the afternoon sunlight. She can smell the comforting aroma of yeast drifting through the kitchen and out into the yard where her father is busy chopping wood for the piche. He was never too busy to answer a question from a child or grandchild running around the yard. Nepefan turned every moment into a teaching opportunity. Dunia can see her husband, Jacob, coming in from the fields, tired and hungry from his labor. He has a satisfied look on his beautiful tanned face.

By early afternoon, Dunia has dug as far down and wide as she can dig. She's done!

Next, she lays a sheet onto the cottage floor, puts her arms under the professor's arms and hoists his body up. She gets his feet onto the sheet, so she can drag him out of the cottage and into the yard. His body is much smaller than when she first arrived but the task is awkward and she has to stop to rest, reposition the sheet and regain her grip. She carries him down toward his grave in increments, praying for his forgiveness for every bump along the way and the general clumsiness of the task.

Once his body is resting in his grave, Dunia pauses to catch her breath. She can hear the gurgle of the river at the bottom of the embankment and the clucking of chickens up toward the cottage. A breeze blows through, rustling the leaves of the oak tree and swaying the grass.

"Don't go anywhere," Dunia says, tongue in cheek, knowing that the professor would take pleasure in such a comment. She turns and walks back up to the cottage for a few items she needs for his burial ceremony.

She returns ready to say her final goodbye.

Dunia puts the locket, the theater program and a bouquet of purple bells onto the professor's body. And then she sings… one final song to put the professor and all of her losses to rest in the ground. She sings Plyve kacha po Tysyni[2].

The song tells a story about a young man calling out to his mother in mourning. He is a soldier that fears that he will die on foreign soil. He asks, "Who will bury me?"

Dunia sings for the professor, and for everyone else she's lost along the way. As she sings, tears stream down her cheeks. A warm breeze blows through the oak tree and rustles the leaves.

When her song is done, she stands in silence for a long time. Then she speaks in prayer, "Dear God," she says, "Help me to let them go."

She takes up her shovel and delves into the massive pile of soft, turned earth. Then she begins the task of burying the professor's body. Her sweat, her tears, the weight of the soil, the power of the ritual frees her from her burdens, her guilt and her sense of responsibility in the loss of her children.

When she's done, the sun has dipped down below the horizon and the light is replaced with the cool blue shades of twilight. Dunia places a small glass jar on top of the grave. Inside is a small piece of paper with the professor's requested epitaph.

There is a tiny and brilliant light burning in the heart of man that will not go out no matter how dark the world becomes. –Leo Tolstoy

---

2. The duckling floats on the Tisina (a river in the Ukraine)

44

THE TRUCK

The professor is in the ground for six weeks before a dark green military truck bounces its way up the driveway. The rain has carved out gouges in the muddy trail and the sun has dried them into hard ruts. The vehicle slows down to a crawl, trying to navigate the path, dipping this way and that. The driver leans forward in his seat and then cranes his head out the window, searching the ground for the smoothest way ahead.

Dunia is chopping wood in the yard when she hears the engine. She pauses, with the ax held up over her head and turns to look toward the sound. The sight of the truck brings a mixture of fear, relief and hope. She has been preparing for winter, gathering food; nuts, berries and mushrooms from the woods, making cheese, reinforcing Anastasia's shed and chopping a mountain of wood. She has begun stacking it up against the side of the cottage, bracing for the first snow-fall, which is probably only a few days away. Dunia didn't know when the officer would come back or if he would come back at all. She needed to prepare for any possibility. Dunia brings the ax down into the stump, wipes the sweat from her brow and watches the truck inch its way toward her. She will have to navigate whatever news this truck brings her, but she may not have to navigate a Russian winter alone in the cottage.

The truck sways back and forth and shudders to a stop, as the driver cuts the engine. An officer gets out of the passenger seat and slams the door behind him. Dunia recognizes him. He is the same officer from the prison; the one that spoke so fondly about the professor and made arrangements for her to come to the cottage and care for him.

"Hello Mother," the young man says, smoothing out the wrinkles in his coat.

Dunia relaxes as she hears the sentiment leave his mouth.

"Hello," she replies.

"Where is he?"

"He's gone...there," Dunia says, pointing to the mound of earth under the oak tree.

The officer nods at her and walks toward the grave.

In the meantime, the driver of the vehicle, an older soldier, has made his way out of the cab and is looking around at the yard.

"Do you want water?" she asks.

"Yes, that would be good," the man says, stretching his back.

Dunia walks toward the well and the man follows, looking around curiously at the property. She pulls up the bucket and the man drinks.

"Good," he says finally after taking a long drink and wiping his mouth on the back of his hand.

"Are you hungry?" Dunia asks.

"Yes, that would be good," he says.

Dunia makes her way back toward the cottage, glancing down toward the grave at the officer who seems to be in conversation with the professor, or maybe in prayer. She leaves him to it.

She prepares a meal; scrambled eggs with cheese and mushrooms, seasoned with wild garlic and sage, and for dessert; wild blueberries and cream, courtesy of Anastasia.

The men eat like they haven't seen food in a while. Dunia is sure they haven't eaten a home cooked meal like this in several years. When they are done, the young officer leans back. He seems more subdued now than he did the day she first overheard his conversation in the prison. When Dunia volunteered to take care of the professor, the officer reacted in anger. Now he's calm.

"When did he die?" he asks, pushing his plate away.

"Six weeks ago," Dunia replies.

"Yes, I thought he must be gone but I couldn't arrange to leave the prison until now."

Dunia nods.

"Did he die in pain?" the officer continues.

"He was a delight and I truly cared for him," Dunia runs her finger around a knot in the grain of the wooden table as she speaks. "He was able to enjoy his books right up until the end and when he couldn't read anymore, I read to him." Dunia says, gesturing toward a stack of books. When Dunia looks back at the officer, she sees that his eyes have a shine to them. The look reminds her of the same look the professor gave her the day she sang to him. She wonders then if this man is, in fact, the professor's son. It would explain both the hardness and the softness within him. Suddenly, Dunia feels a deepened connection with the man."He went peacefully one rainy afternoon. I don't think he was in great pain. His body just slowly shut down, as old bodies do."

After this, they sit in silence for a long time. The driver is looking down at his hand resting on his full belly. He has a look of quiet contentment on his face and his lips are slightly blue in the corners, from the blueberries.

Dunia smiles.

"Thank you for taking care of him," the officer says.

"Yes, of course," Dunia says, "I am grateful for it."

Time goes on. Dunia cleans up the table, stokes the fire in the stove and adds fresh wood as the evening chill sets in.

"We'll stay here tonight and then tomorrow we will leave this place," the officer announces.

Dunia nods. She doesn't ask any questions.

The next morning they are up early. Dunia milks Anastasia for the last time. She makes sure the cow is off her lead, so she is free to wander. She doesn't know what will happen to her now that she's leaving. Anastasia's fate is in God's hands. Dunia runs her hand along the cow's warm flank.

"Maahh!" Dunia says.

Anastasia turns her head and looks at her with a soft and gentle gaze.

"Who will milk you?" She asks quietly, her face nestled near the cow's ear. "I must leave now, my dear."

Dunia pats the cow and heads back to the cottage to gather a few things. The truck is already warming up. Dunia dumps the last of the chicken feed in the yard. The chickens gather in a frenzy.

"Good luck ladies," she says, her breath coming out as a puff of white steam in the frosty air. Then she opens the shed door, offering them a place to hide from the winter. "We all have to find our own way to survive," she continues. She knows that the snow and cold are not far off. Dunia stands back and takes one final look at the cottage before climbing up into the passenger seat of the military truck. The officer follows her in and slams the door behind him. She is now sandwiched between officer and driver. She clutches a small bag of her belongings.

"Let's go," the officer says.

The driver nods and the truck lurches forward, pulling a u-turn and heading back out the way it came. Dunia looks wistfully at the mound of earth under the oak tree and then settles back into her seat. The morning drizzle has thickened up in the cold and lands as sleet on the windshield. They traverse a maze of country roads before they finally reach a main road and turn east. They are headed in the direction of Dunia's homeland.

45

THE AUTHORITIES, 1939

Dunia has served 7 years of her 11 year sentence.

"Come with me!" the guard says, banging his baton against the prison bars. The noise reverberates and echoes down the hall.

Dunia and her cell mate look at each other and then back at the guard, unsure of which of them he's talking to.

"You," he says pointing his baton at Dunia, "Come with me right now."

Dunia gets up to follow the man.

"Bring your stuff. You won't be back" he says, examining his baton in the fluorescent light, taking in its glossy, black sheen and trying out its slap in the palm of his hand.

Dunia turns and looks at her cell mate's face, as if the meaning of the guard's words might be found there. The woman stares back wide-eyed. Dunia is afraid.

"Let's go," the man says impatiently.

Dunia grabs her bundle off of the bed and walks toward the door.

"Goodbye," she says to the woman. Her name is Katya, the same as Dunia's mother. Dunia has only known her for two weeks. It's amazing how quickly you can get to know someone when sharing such a small space and in the midst of such uncertainty. What the woman didn't say directly during the day, was evident in the haunting words that she cried out at night. Dunia felt as gray as the walls before the guard came in and called her to come out. Now her face is white as snow as she follows the man down the hallway and out of the prison wing.

A prisoner stands in her cell, grimy fingers with long curved nails, curled around the prison bars. She screams as Dunia walks by, "You're gonna die, you're gonna die, you're gonna die!"

"Shut your filthy mouth!!" the guard shouts, returning to bang his baton on the bars of the woman's cell and smashing her fingers.

The woman cries out in pain and recoils back into the depths of her cell.

Dunia squeezes her eyes shut for a moment while every part of her being contracts.

'I can't look and I can't feel,' she thinks to herself.

The man continues. He leads her through the mess hall to a set of locked doors. Dunia can hear the sounds of a meal being prepared in the kitchen.

"Set those down here," a cook in the kitchen shouts out over the clang and clatter of pots. The distinct odor of rotten meat is drifting through the hall.

"Open up!" the guard shouts, banging his baton on the door and gesturing to another guard seated behind a desk in a closed booth. With a hard stare, the man looks out at them through a small circular window. He presses a button to unlock the doors, allowing them to pass through.

Dunia's heart is pounding now and her legs move forward of their own volition. She moves as though in a dream and wonders, 'Is this the way I am to die?'

'God have mercy,' she prays, 'God have mercy,' she continues, saying the words over and over again, in her mind.

She follows the man down another hall and while it is still drab and colorless, it feels very different from the hall she just came from. The change is palpable. Everything looks the same and yet the feeling is very different.

'What is it?' Dunia thinks, pondering the unmistakable change in atmosphere.

'It's quiet,' she realizes at last. The sound of guards shouting orders, batons banging against prison bars, and prisoner's howling in agony has disappeared. 'It's quiet,' Dunia repeats in her mind. She breathes.

'One thing at a time,' she thinks, 'You're alive...you can keep walking...one foot in front of the other."

In the sudden silence, Dunia's mind clears. Over the past few weeks in prison, bits of information have filtered to her ears. Despite the guards' harshness, they haven't been careful with their words. The political landscape is shifting, stirring an urgent need for conversation. She's overheard soldiers—sometimes whispering, other times engaging in heated discussions that spill into the night, when the prisoners are supposed to be asleep. Power is in motion. Leaders are repositioning themselves, and the soldiers, officers, and guards are tense, restless, bracing for what lies ahead. Stalin and Hitler have signed the Nazi-Soviet pact. Why two former political enemies would align is unclear. *They must believe there's power to be gained from their alliance,* Dunia thinks, as she walks down the long hallway. The thought lingers, unsettling and inescapable.

Dunia breathes deeply. The man comes to a thick wooden door and knocks twice. A muffled voice responds from the other side. Dunia is pushed through the door with the hard tip of the baton between her shoulder blades. Inside the room there are three men seated behind a glossy wooden table.

"Sit there," one of the men, an officer in a green military coat, says to her, pointing to the lone chair in front of the long table.

Dunia sits and looks at the men. In one glance, she can see which one is in charge. He is an older man, broad shouldered with a thick sweep of dark hair, graying at the temples. He's wearing a navy blazer with various stripes and decorations to indicate his importance. He hasn't spoken yet, but his hands are clasped under his chin. He watches Dunia take a seat and then looks her over with a cold stare.

Dunia can't look back at the man. She knows that this man has the power to crush her. She looks down and grips her bundle furiously to hide the tremble in her hands.

The man speaks. "Everything you have seen and everywhere you have been, I want you to forget about it." he pauses to let his words sink in. "Nothing happened here, do you understand?" he says looking at her, his eyes unblinking.

Dunia looks back at him now, listening carefully but unable to absorb his meaning.

'Is he talking about here in this room, or here in the prison?' she thinks. She hasn't eaten a proper meal in two weeks and her mind feels foggy and muddled.

"Do you hear me?" he says insistently, "I want you to forget everything you saw and everything you experienced. It was nothing but a dream, do you understand?"

Dunia understands now and stares back, hoping her face doesn't reveal the impossibility of his request.

"You forget and you don't tell anyone," the man says, "Or else we will find you and we will kill you, your family, your children. Do you understand?"

Dunia cringes at the mention of her children. She knows that some of them are already dead. At this she feels hatred rising up from her gut. She wants to throw up. But instead she swallows. She has swallowed so much shit over the past seven years that it's like an old habit.

"Do you hear me, woman? I need you to answer me," he shouts and slams his fist on the table.

"It is forgotten," Dunia says numbly. Looking briefly into the man's eyes, trying to convey her understanding and conceal her murderous rage.

"It is forgotten," she says again, looking down at her feet.

The man continues to look at her. Dunia's heart feels like it is pounding out of her chest and she focuses her eyes on a dark stain on the floor in front of her chair.

'Is that blood?' she thinks.

Finally the man looks away. He signs a paper that is laid out on the table before him.

"Your sentence has been served, you are free to go," he says, handing the paperwork to the guard.

It takes all of Dunia's energy to contain her reaction to these words; she wants to yell and scream, she wants to tear these men into a million pieces, she wants to fall on her knees and weep. But instead she gathers her bundle and stands up.

"Thank you," she says and then turns to follow the prison guard back out the way she came.

'It's over, it's over, it's over,' she says to herself in disbelief.

As she passes back through the mess hall, there are several officers gathered there. Among them, she sees the professor's son. The group is caught up in conversation. Dunia makes eye contact with the man for a fleeting moment. An understanding passes between them.

Thank you, Dunia thinks, as she walks by.

The guard takes her to an office where she is given an envelope with her release papers and enough money to catch a train. Then he leads her out toward the main door.

"Go on," he says, pointing the baton down the asphalt path away from the prison.

'I know where that baton belongs,' Dunia thinks, her rage still churning. She steps out into the cold November morning and walks away. She walks quickly, afraid that they will change their mind. Afraid that someone will come running after her and tell her that a mistake has been made and that she has to finish the rest of her sentence in the gulag. Once she has walked a mile or so and the prison is out of sight, the tears begin to flow. They roll down her cheeks, under her chin and into the woolen collar of her sweater. She lets them fall. She's free. And she's going home.

46

THE SEARCH

Dunia rests on a bench in a small sunny courtyard in the city of Dnepropetrovsk. The cobbled square is lined with pear trees and they are in full blossom. A breeze blows through the courtyard, lifting fallen petals upward and whirling them around like a warm and fragrant snow-storm. A quarrel of sparrows dart in and out around her feet, looking for crumbs. Dunia shifts, adjusting her skirt and the birds startle, flying off in one unified flutter.

Dunia hasn't returned to Kobeliaky yet. She can't. After all the turmoil she has been through, after years of trying to get there, she's afraid to go back. She's afraid to go home, afraid of what she'll find or won't find, afraid of the silence within the walls of her house. 'I need to know that at least one of my children is still alive before I go back.'

That's not the only thing that kept her tethered to the city. When Dunia arrived in Dnepropetrovsk, winter had set in and the road to Kobeliaky was cold and uninviting for a woman with no money and no means of traveling, besides her feet. So she chose to stay. Stay and earn some money while gathering the tattered edges of her life together. It also gave her an opportunity to look for her children. 'If my children are alive, it makes sense that they would come to the city for work.'

Dunia found a job cleaning. It's a humble job but she doesn't mind. After prison, the freedom to work in silence and go home to a safe place at the end of the day carries its own bliss. The work also gives her time to think about the past. She feels a strange sense of satisfaction in bringing order to one small, untidy corner of the world. Dunia found a place to stay with three other women in a grimy complex that had inadvertently become a half-way house for women. They are women recovering from war, from losing children, from unjust sentences and from the loss of their lives as they knew them.

Dunia takes every opportunity she can to share about her children. What they look like, what their names are, what they might be wearing. She's been gone so long that she is going on very little. But she can't stop searching. It has become an obsession.

"And her name is Marta," she says to an old woman selling wares along Topolya street. The old woman looks at her with concern after listening patiently to the long description of Dunia's daughter.

"I see a lot of people," the old woman replies, "And every mother is looking for her children right now."

Dunia looks down, rubbing her fingertips into her temples.

She knows the odds are against her but she can't seem to stop.

"I'll keep my eyes open," the woman continues, her eyes softening.

It was the end of the workday and Dunia was walking home thinking, 'I'll just talk to one more person.' The conversation feels like another dead end.

Dunia has felt moments of hopelessness throughout the winter. It has brought her to her knees. But the spring brings new life. Dunia waits on the bench with renewed hope and purpose. One of her friends has seen a man matching Ivan's description eating lunch with a group of men in the courtyard for the past few weeks.

"The men wander in around noon. They must work around there," the friend had said.

Dunia arrives early and she waits in reserved anticipation, preparing for disappointment. She has to preserve her hopes and release them in measured doses. She knows that she may have to give up her search soon and go back to Kobeliaky. The weather has improved and she has become strong enough now that she could travel the road on foot or pay someone to take her home.

As Dunia waits, she prays. Her mind wanders back to the island of Prorva, to Asim, the man with the amber eyes. She can remember the first time she saw him and how far apart their worlds seemed then. 'Our paths were destined to intertwine,' she thinks, 'neither of us had control over that.' Dunia remembers the words he spoke to her while she was unconscious - the beautiful stream of prayers that surrounded her during her darkest hours. She recites his prayer now. She doesn't know the language but she forms the sounds by heart. She prays out loud, letting the "words" wash over her. They spill from her mouth down onto the bench and overflow all around her into the flower carpeted courtyard, like curling tendrils of light. Dunia knows that she would have died on that island without his help. He is far away now, living his own life but she knows that when she bows her head, they both pray to the same God.

Dunia sees him now; a vision. He's walking down a winding trail through the woods with Saleema at his side, her clever eyes scanning the forest floor for berries and herbs. Niazmina and Rakeem follow behind like ducklings. Rakeem is carrying a gnarled stick in front of him like a dagger and talking to himself, some story about a djinn playing out in his imagination. She sees them down by the shore. Asim casts his net into the sparkling sea and Rakeem looks on, bent over, scanning the water for movement. Saleema is crouched down with the sun on her back, lighting a fire among the rocks while Niazmina chases the wind, arms aloft, green scarf trailing out behind her.

Dunia remembers suddenly that the green scarf isn't on the island anymore. It's tucked away, down deep among her belongings, a gift from the child. She's kept it hidden away all this time and nearly forgotten about it. 'When I get to my home, I'll wear it with pride,' she thinks.

She's pulled from her vision by the voices of men. She can't see them yet, but she can hear the deep roll of their conversation in the distance. A group of them enter the courtyard from the south side. Dunia is up on her feet, scanning their faces, looking desperately for one that she recognizes.

"Ivan! Ivan!" she screams, holding out her arms. The men startle and look at her, wondering if she's mad. Then there is recognition and her son steps forward, shocked by the sight of her here, alive in front of him.

He looks lean and strong. The soft roundness of his cheeks is gone, replaced by angles and dark stubble. When she looks at his face, she can see traces of Jacob there. Ivan's eyes look different; deep, strong and steady. She sees his pain there too. These eyes have seen a lot. She feels an ache in her heart, wishing, suddenly, that she could have protected him from everything. He is wearing a brown wool jacket, unbuttoned down the front, open to the warmth of the day, revealing a white cotton shirt underneath.

"Mama?" he says questioningly, as if he might be talking to a ghost. "Mama," he repeats, stepping closer, arms held toward her and tears in his eyes. Dunia wonders what he sees when he looks at her. She tries to read it in his gaze. She feels like an old woman, even though she is only 44.

The men draw back. Under different circumstances they might have given Ivan a hard time about what happened next. But these men understand the separation and loss of war and each one has suffered their own version of it.

Mother and son embrace, Dunia kisses her son's cheeks and presses her forehead into his. *He is a grown man but he still smells like my son*, she thinks.

"Dad's dead," he says, "And so is Mary."

Dunia hears him and accepts what she already knows. "Ok," she says, squeezing his shoulders, "I'm so sorry." She doesn't know why she's apologizing. She just feels so sorry for his loss and pain -even though she shares in the same loss. She carries the burden doubly, once for herself and once more for her beloved son. Perhaps on some level, she is sorry for bringing him into this world only to suffer. The burden of being a mother. *I was supposed to protect you,* she thinks.

Then she holds his forearms and looks into his face. "Here you are," she says, "I have never stopped looking for you." They embrace again, trembling and sobbing.

"You're alive Mama," he says, "I can't believe you're alive."

"Yes, I know."

"What happened?" he asks.

"I'll tell you," she replies.

EPILOGUE

If you wander down an old weather-beaten trail through the woods near Kobeliaky, the path opens up into a wide green field. It's over-grown with wildflowers and herbs; mint, parsley and sage. In the distance sits a small squat cottage. White smoke curls lazily skyward from the chimney. There are massive sunflowers planted along its southern wall; their leaves are yellow with a kiss of red in the center. Their heads are turned toward the sun and stretch as high as the roof. To the west, a garden bursts with late summer produce; cabbage, beets, kohlrabi, carrots and beans, their vines climbing upwards, twisting round and round a sturdy trellis tower. In the far corner is an assortment of exotic spices; cardamom, paprika and saffron. They are not native to this area but seem to be flourishing.

The path between the rows of vegetables has been tamped down by several sets of footprints. It has rained recently, so the soil is moist and holds the perfect shape of a bare foot. One set of footprints belongs to an old woman and another to her daughter. Together they picked vegetables for a meal and marveled over the size of the rhubarb plant at the other end of the garden. You could almost take shelter under its leaves on a sunny afternoon. They harvested some of this too, for dessert.

If you look closely, there are also smaller sets of footprints. One belongs to a little girl, five years old, and another, more wobbly set, belongs to a little boy. He is just learning how to walk. Sometimes you can see his feet, set wide apart for balance, and at other times his little handprints mark the place where he lost his balance and tumbled forward.

It's morning now and the garden is quiet. The smell of baking bread wafts out of the cottage door which is propped open with a metal pail. Inside you can hear the sound of a woman humming. A yellow finch sits in the apple tree nearby and chirps out his morning song with abandon. The woman sings her response.

A REQUEST

Thank you for being here.

If you enjoyed the story, I would be incredibly grateful if you could take a moment to leave a review on Amazon.

As a small independent publisher, your positive feedback means the world to me. Reviews not only support my work but also help me continue doing what I love; creating more stories for readers like you to enjoy.

Here's a QR code-

Thank you so much for your support!

Warm regards,
Gillian Caldwell

WORDS OF GRATITUDE

I want to express my deepest gratitude to everyone who helped transform this book from a mere thought, a tiny seed of conception, into a tangible reality.

Thank you to Gabriela and Vanessa for sharing in our writers' group and offering invaluable feedback on my early chapters. Your insights were instrumental.

To my sister, Alanna, thank you for beta reading the book in its final stages—your sharp eye and mind like a steel trap caught every detail.

I am profoundly grateful to my ancestors, who were with me throughout this creative journey, offering their wisdom and guidance.

To my dad, Russ, your quiet, humble, and steadfast support has meant the world to me. Even in the background, your presence never went unnoticed.

And a very special thank you to my mother, Annie. You have been with me every step of the way, offering encouragement, insights, and wisdom, and generously sharing pieces of our family history to help bring this vision to life. I truly couldn't have done it without you.

Thank you, thank you, thank you!

AUTHOR BIO

Gillian Caldwell has always had a deep love for words. From a young age, she found joy in crafting poetry, weaving stories, and offering prayers to the Universe. Her passion for storytelling began with her mother, who introduced her to the magic of narratives during their hikes in the Rocky Mountains. At just five years old, when little Gillian grew tired and sat down on the trail in tears, her mother would extend a hand and say, "Come on, I'll tell you a story." Those stories transformed their hikes into joyful adventures, creating cherished memories and igniting a lifelong appreciation for the power of words. She studied Journalism in Calgary, where she honed her skills in writing and narrative craft. Dunia - A Garden in the Gulag is Gillian's debut novel, a heartfelt tribute to her family's history and the enduring power of resilience and faith. Through her writing, she seeks to connect with readers, paint the landscape and share stories that inspire and resonate on a deeply human level.

www.ingramcontent.com/pod-product-compliance
Lightning Source LLC
Chambersburg PA
CBHW031255120726
47906CB00003B/755

* 9 7 8 1 0 6 9 3 2 9 8 6 8 *